# After The

# HOLY GHOST

# YE SHALL RECEIVE POWER

## Pastor Gregory Link

## *PGL Ministries*

*"Healing Hearts, and Saving Souls through the Power of God"*

After The Holy Ghost, Ye Shall Receive Power

Copyright © 2018 by Gregory Link

Printed in the United States of America

Unless otherwise indicated, all Scripture quotations are used from the King James, and the New International Versions of the Bible.

For more information, address:

PGL Ministries

125 Arnett Blvd. Unit 12-B

Danville, VA 24541

(434) 709-0080

First Printing, 2018

ISBN 978-1535408653

# Contents

# Dedication

*"In the beginning was the Word, and the Word was with God, and the Word was God."* John 1:1

First, and foremost, I would like to give the glory, and honor to God for allowing my story, and testimate to be manifested. I am just a willing vessel, and God is truly the author and finisher of this book. I am a living witness of the Holy Ghost, and have poured out my heart to testify to the power of the Almighty. As I have experienced the last 18 years of trials, and tribulations, with some of it being good, and some bad I give all praise to my Father for His humbling grace and mercy. I would like to thank my family and friends who went along with me on this journey, although some may not have been aware of how God was transforming my life, but still stood by my side. Special thanks to Sylvia Hairston, and Tarlene Wilson for your dedication and support towards building my vision. Lastly, I would like to sincerely thank my cousin, Kawauna McElroy for all of your hard work that was put in behind the scenes to make this book project come into fruition. **I am beyond grateful for everyone in my life.**

## As My Journey Begins

As I sit here in the bathroom reading a book "Manifesting the Divine Nature" by Smith Wigglesworth, I began to think of myself and the supernatural power of revelations that had been revealed to me by the Holy Spirit. This awakening challenged me to travel down memory lane, which led me back to my childhood. At that time, I began to connect the dots of my life. During those years, there were a lot of supernatural manifestations that took place, which I could not understand. I would continuously have unexplainable dreams, and visions. Being without full understanding, I didn't question much. Deep down I felt that there was something different about me; I just couldn't quite put my finger on it. What I knew was that one day I was probably going to be used by the Lord, but I just didn't know how.

Even as a young boy, I didn't really play like normal kids did. I was a fun and vibrant boy, but old soul at heart. I would go around to the different elders that were sitting on their porches and talk to them. I felt in my spirit that they needed someone to talk to and pray with. Looking back now, I realize that I was doing evangelist work. Although I had plenty of siblings, and friends to play with, I still related more to my elders. I was intrigued with the many lessons they gave, and teaching principles that they instilled in me.

Even then, I didn't connect the dots to my purpose and calling.

As I grew older, I began to see the works of the power of the Almighty. I would see things that people weren't able to see, but I wouldn't share with anyone, because I was afraid that they would look at me as if I was out of my mind. I would see shadows and different types of figures. I couldn't figure out what they were, but I saw these objects. I wasn't afraid of what I was seeing, but it brought something down on the inside of me that made me hesitant. Later it was revealed to me that I was seeing spirits. What stood out to me most of all was that even as a young man, I've always had faith. I really never had the spirit of fear. The spirit of faith allowed me to believe in God. I didn't look at anything thinking that it was impossible, I've always looked at life that all things are possible, through Christ. This immeasurable level of faith led me to be the man that I am today, and I am truly humbled.

It was at that moment that I finally understood that in life, not everyone is going to understand the power of The

Holy Spirit, unless there is a divine connection between them and God. Therefore, I ask you to read this book with a clear understanding, knowing that our Father is the creator of this world, and that there is nothing too hard for God. Notice that I said, "God" and not Greg.

You see, as a follower, a believer, and a true Christian, I will be the first to admit that I, Gregory Link do not have any power to do anything without the Creator. For without the Most High, nothing would exist, not even myself. He is the King of Kings, the Great I AM, the Alpha and Omega. I am simply a vessel, willing to be used by Him. I am not here to exalt myself. I only have a burning desire for testifying to the supernatural experiences that the Lord has delivered, and the manifestations that came to pass. In the chapters to come, you will read that throughout my life, I've undergone an out of body experience, casted out demonic spirits, saw signs and wonders of the sun, the wind, and even the rain. I've been blessed to receive the power of the Almighty to heal people. To God be all of the Glory! It is my prayer and hope that you will become equipped with the understanding of healing, deliverance, and ultimately empowered to receive the Holy Spirit just as I have.

I wrote this book, because there are believers under the assumption that they have the Holy Ghost, but there is no true evidence of the power. I've always said to myself, if God has given you the gift of healing, the gift of casting out demonic spirits, then there should be evidence and proof that God has given you the authority. Not by His power, but He has given you the authority to use His power to work for Him as a servant. I believe that there are more unbelievers in this world than true believers. Whether your beliefs are of little faith, or non-existent, once God begins to reveal revelations to you, your belief and your faith will become unmeasured. That's a promise.

Besides, what better a person to be used to show how God can call on as me? Don't get it twisted, I will be the first to admit that I too once was lost, and now I am found. From playing baseball, to rapping, to being a professional dancer, and then dabbling in stand-up comedy, I never thought in a million years that I was called to preach God's word. Me of all people? You've got to be playing right? It took some time of wondering in the wilderness, but God shut that stuff down, only for me to fulfill my true and anointed purpose in life. Nevertheless, it was all a part of God's plan. Some things I regret doing, and some things I'm happy that I was able to experience those life lessons. All in all, giving my life to Christ was the best decision that I have ever made in my life. All that I can say is thank God for redemption and deliverance. God did it for me, and I know that He can do the same for you!

After my younger years, and into adulthood, there was a period in my life where I really didn't believe. God had to make me out to be a believer in order for me to really start working for Him. I had the spirit of disbelief, saying "God you have to show me, better than you can tell me". Once He began to show His word, I was won over, and never questioned Him again. Psalm 37:4 says: "Delight yourself in the Lord, and He will give you the desires of your heart." Once God began revealing super natural things to me, I started to develop a desiring spirit and appetite for God to give me more. Matthew 5:6 says: "Blessed are those who hunger and thirst for righteousness, for they will be filled. Oh, taste and see that the Lord is good!"

I needed a supernatural teaching to elevate the spirit of God. I was shown messages in the supernatural realm that only He could reveal to me, in a way that no man ever could. Now, I'm not saying that Man cannot teach me anything, but when it comes to the evidence of the true power of God, I hunger, and I thirst for true, divine, supernatural substance. Once the Lord begins to show you His word in the supernatural realm, nothing on the natural level satisfies your hunger. He has proven countless times that He is real, He is who He says that He is, and that there is no other God besides Him. I believe that He is able to do all things, and that He has all the power.

Throughout this book, you will also learn more in depth of how the Holy Spirit can operate in your life, allowing you access to God's power. This will ultimately help us build the Kingdom. In the day and time that we live in, the world needs more people of radical faith, equipped to operate in His divine power to help save lost souls and non-believers. Just as many of us have experienced the wilderness during our season of transition, I needed a divine encounter, and a word from God. I was once a non-believer, but had faith the size of a mountain. I came to realize that faith will move mountains, but believing will allow you to see it move. I never doubted God. I just needed Him to prove to me that all things were possible, and once He did, my life began to change. I hope that my story and teachings will inspire you to believe in the power, and the blood.

## My Divine Encounter: Out of Body Experience

One evening, I was lying across the bed of my hotel room after a work assignment. It was in that hour that I felt my spirit leave my body, and the Lord revealed to me Hell. It was hot, chaotic, and on fire. People were screaming for help, and I could literally feel my heart beating out of my chest. It was complete, total darkness, but was never ending. After hearing the voice of the Lord saying: "Well, this too shall come to pass, but you also have the gift of healing according to your faith." After that encounter, I could then feel my spirit enter back into my body, and my hands began tremble. I sat up in the bed and began to cry like a baby. I can vividly remember how I immediately took my diamond earrings out of my ear and started walking around in the room and pacing back and forth all night. I stayed up the entire evening, and for the first time in my life was terrified. I was so afraid that I could not lie back down. Even though I feared what God would expose to me next, I was made a believer that night! I believe the blood still works; it's just like fire shut up in my bones!

## The First Evidence of the Healing Power

When June, my brother who was sharing a hotel room with me for work finally woke up, I felt compelled to share what had happened. I normally would keep strange things to myself just as in the past, but this was much different. This direct encounter had shaken me to the core. I said "Listen, man. You will never believe what happened to me. I just had an out of body experience. The Lord said that I had the gift of healing." He said "Yeah, right. Mmm....yeah, whatever." I didn't become offended, because just as I had been a nonbeliever at times, I wouldn't expect him to not think that I was crazy. I simply replied: "Well, okay" and I left it at that. I knew that it wasn't my place to convince him, but it was my assignment to speak about my experience with the Almighty. A few days later, I was walking past him at work, and noticed that he was slumped over. I rushed over to see what was wrong with him, and in extreme pain, he yelled for someone to call an ambulance. He could feel a knot in his side the size of a softball. I just looked at him. He pleaded with me to see for myself, and to touch it. The minute I reached out to touch the knot, it left his body. June rose up, and he looked at me in bewilderment of what had just happened. It was amazingly gone. I was turning about to leave, and he asked me not to go anywhere in case it came back. When I turned back around, out of nowhere I said: "God said, not so. He had to make a believer out of you, because you did not believe when I told you I had the gift of healing." I walked away, and the softball size knot never returned in his body. To this day, my brother testifies about how he was healed, saying: "If I didn't see it for myself, I wouldn't have believed it. He revealed to me these things for himself. There's proof and evidence, and I am the witness." He is now a believer of God's power. Glory to God!

Pictured here is my brother, witness and believer, William a.k.a. "June"

# CHAPTER 1

## What Does The Holy Ghost Do?

*"The Holy Spirit does many things in the lives of believers."*

*A Helper (John 14:26)*

We, as Believers – Christians – are supposed to be the light of the world, shining in the darkness, we are supposed to be the calm in the storm. Christ came to the world in human form to show the way, and when He was departing, He did not leave us empty; He left us with the Holy Ghost. In my opinion, I think that we have lost sight of this precious gift, and ultimately lost sight of Christ himself.

When our Lord and Savior was ascending into heaven, He knew He had to leave His followers with something that would serve as a daily guide and a companion to them. The Bible today is our number one guide, it tells us about the expectation of God on our lives and how we can journey through this sinful world without becoming of the world. The Holy Spirit is our constant Helper and Comforter; He reveals to us things that are to come.

*My Spirit comes with the Spirit of wisdom, understanding, counsel, might, knowledge, and fear of the Lord. When My Spirit moves, all these attributes come with Me. It is not by your own power but by the power of My Spirit.*

Would you believe that many of us live our lives in ignorance and blindness, even after Jesus had given us the ultimate guide to daily living and survival? Those of us who profess Christ, and still struggle with this are no better off than unbelievers; this is because we have no idea what we live for or what the future holds for us. The scripture says, "The Holy Spirit will reveal all things" (John 16:13); if indeed the Holy Spirit reveals all things, then we should never be ignorant. If the Holy Spirit is going to teach you everything, that means you know things before they ever happen; they are confirmed to you in the spiritual realm. Just think about how we deal with the adversary. Too many of us fall into the trap of the devil, being ignorant to the fact that anyone who is filled with the Holy Spirit is never susceptible to the devices of the devil. Satan's job is to have you thinking that God is not a healer, and that the blood doesn't work. The Holy Spirit does a lot of things in the life of anyone who believes. Now, before we dive into the things that the Holy Spirit does, let's take a brief look at the Holy Spirit, and attempt to explain it.

## Holy Spirit

The Holy Spirit is an important part of the Christian trinity; God the Father, God the Son and God the Holy Spirit. Often times, our attention is centered on God the Father and God the Son, leaving out the Holy Spirit. However, the Holy Spirit is just as important as every other member of the trinity. In fact, the Bible emphasizes that all sins can be forgiven, but blasphemy against the Holy Spirit is unforgivable (Matthew 12:30-32, Mark 3:28-30 and Luke 12:8-10). We must constantly guide our mouths and our hearts, in order to keep it holy; the Holy Spirit does not dwell in a heart that is full of filth, bitterness or hate. Only love.

Even though the Holy Spirit has always been in existence since the beginning of time, it was not until Jesus departed that it began to manifest in the lives of those who believed in Him. The Bible itself starts with; "in the beginning God created the heaven and the earth, and the earth was without form, and void; and darkness was upon the face of the deep. And the Spirit of God moved upon the face of the waters" (Genesis 1:1-2). The Spirit of God, in which the Bible refers to is the same that guides all believers today. It is more of an ever-present presence; with Christ leaving with the promise of sending a Helper that will teach all things to his followers. As long as we believe, we are entitled to be filled by the Holy Spirit.

*Learn from Me. I am gentle and lovely in heart....*

In John 16:7, Jesus said: "Nevertheless I tell you the truth; it is to your advantage that I go away; for if I go not away, the Helper will not come to you; but if I depart, I will send him unto you." John 14:26 says "He will teach you all things". Because of what His word says, a believer who has the Holy Spirit should never be stung by the bee of ignorance. It is important to allow the Holy Spirit to teach us all things.

When Christ was alive, he knew all things. Whenever the Pharisees came to him with their tricky questions and tests, Jesus always had the perfect response for them. This gift and ability to know, and to be able to discern all things has been given to us by Christ through the Holy Spirit, and it is available to everyone as long as you believe.

*When I came to your world, though I am God, I did not think of equality with God as something to cling to. I was focused on what My Father has called Me to do. It was not easy because you have to remember that I had a physical body with its limitations. This is why I understand you perfectly.*

The Holy Spirit is God's power in action. It is the third person in the Trinity. He is a Spirit that dwells in the heart of all believers. The reason why we do not see and experience enough of the manifestation of the Holy Spirit in our lives today is because we are not committed enough to the Lord. We surrender to God only with our lips and our tongues, or maybe even just when trouble arises, but our heart is still very far away from Him. In order for us to experience the full power of the Holy Spirit, we must be able to let go of our heart and surrender it to our beloved Yahweh.

*When you reach the end of your own abilities, My Spirit moves! This is what waiting upon me is all about. This is how you renew your strength, the strength that comes from My Spirit. It is the strength that replaces your own, and which comes when you surrender to me because you know you can't do it on your own.*

## How Can The Holy Ghost Help Us?

The Holy Ghost performs many actions in our lives, and it is only those of us who believe that will get to see Him work wonders in us, and through us. As the Bible says, the Holy Ghost is our helper, a helper that works out all of our issues for us. Imagine you have a friend who has the power of the Holy Ghost, and who is always with you, would you ever suffer from anything? Definitely not, this friend would always be there to bail you out whenever there is danger, he would be there to prepare with you when you are about to write that exam – revealing things that are to come – he would be there to lift you up whenever you fell, he would basically be there for whatever you would like him to do. This shows us just how powerful the Holy Spirit is, and how useful He is to our daily existence.

A Bible scholar once said: "many are the gifts of God, but none is greater than the gift of the Holy Spirit. The Spirit is a Comforter, Helper and Counselor for the committed follower of Jesus Christ." This shows us in clear terms why everyone needs this Spirit. It is unfortunate that we may fail in our relationships, we make mistakes, our businesses crumble, and our families may even get torn apart. In all of this turmoil, we sometimes forget that we have the Holy

Spirit who can teach us how to put things in order. Many marriages, and relationships would still be intact had we allowed the Holy Spirit to guide our actions. So many of us are deeply stricken with endless grief, enduring depression, and my even be battling a chronic illness; in all of this adversity, we may not remember to call on the Comforter who can give us joy and peace. I believe that the world is in so much chaos, because we have failed to recognize the presence of the Helper who Christ sent to us.

If you are truly serious about healing, and deliverance, God will get serious with you. If you are not getting healed and delivered, it's not because the Holy Spirit lacks the power to do it. Could it be that you are not serious enough? Seriousness requires total surrender to the process of healing, as well as maintaining your deliverance. It also requires total obedience to what the Holy Spirit shows you. The Holy Spirit will always point you back to the Word of God. One day I believe that you are going to wake up before it is too late. Once you tap into God's divine power, you'll be able to live out a blessed and purposeful life, free of strife and long suffering. I believe in the power of God, just know that He is turning your life all around. A Way Maker He Is!

*"Not by might, nor by power, but by My Spirit. It is My Spirit who will complete what I have asked you to start. It is My Spirit who will stir up that seed you sowed into that person. It is My Spirit who will send the increase to your ministry. It is My Spirit who will create the change in your spouse. It is My Spirit who will lead your children to Me. It is My Spirit who will do the things that look almost impossible for you to accomplish.*

## Indwelling of the Holy Ghost

In order for the Holy Ghost to indwell in us, we must give our lives to Christ whole-heartedly. In the Old Testament, the Spirit of the Lord did not stay with the Israelites; it would come and go, empowering those who He had chosen for his work, and then returning to the Father. However, with the death of Jesus, and the access granted, believers too have a direct access to the Father, we all have become chosen by God. In the book of John 1:12, the Bible says that: "but as many as received Him, to them He gave the right to become children of God, to those who believe in His name." This establishes the authority and the power that believers have in the power of Jesus. It shows how important it is to believe in the King of Kings, and thereby be a child of God. On the other hand, anyone who submits to the works of the devil is not of God, and thereby not entitled to the power of the Holy Spirit. If you want to enjoy the benefits that come with having the Holy Spirit dwell inside of you, then you must choose God ahead of the devil and all ungodliness.

The indwelling of the Holy Ghost is when someone opens their heart in order to allow God to come in and take permanent residence in their body. The Holy Spirit will not come into you unless certain requirements are met. When an unbeliever accepts Christ, the person is not just accepting Christ alone, but the trinity as a whole. Through the confession of Jesus Christ, the Holy Spirit goes into the heart of a new believer to continue to dwell. Being a new believer, it is hard to find your grounding. With the Holy Spirit, your journey becomes easier as it guides you through every step of the way.

It is important to know that anyone who claims to be a born again Christian, yet does not have the Holy Spirit is not truly born again. The Holy Spirit is a gift freely given to all of us at the point of confessing and accepting the Lordship of Jesus. As you grow in faith, you will start to uncover and discover some hidden blessings, and will start to tap into some gifts and promises of the spirit.

When you experience the indwelling of the Holy Spirit, you will become a bona fide child of God. The Holy Spirit will guide you gradually into full maturity in the journey of faith. As Jesus rightly said, the world is full of tribulations, and being children of God does not make us immune to the tribulations. With the presence of the Holy Spirit, we can easily weather any storm, and overcome any tribulation you face. Just take a look at the lives of us believers; despite the fact that we tapped directly from Jesus, we are still faced several tribulations. We want to walk with Christ only when it is all good, but the moment it becomes tough, we take a step back. Know that we are going to face the good, the bad, and the ugly when we walk with Christ. The Holy Spirit is there to prepare us for whatever is to come. Just remember that God never said that the weapons wouldn't form, but that they won't prosper. As the Holy Spirit dwells and lives in us, here are some things that will start to manifest:

## The Acquisition of the Spiritual Gifts

As the Holy Spirit starts to dwell in the lives of us, we begin to acquire spiritual gifts. Spiritual gifts are abilities and graces in which God gives to believers that yearn for them, for the purpose of the kingdom. These gifts are different from talents or fruits of the spirit, and it is different from the gift of the Holy Spirit. Spiritual gifts are meant for the advancement of the gospel, and the edification of the church. They are not for personal use.

There are a lot of people who are spiritually gifted, but we unknowingly have resistance towards using them. What happens is that we know that we are gifted but are afraid to use our gifts. When God has given you a gift, he wants you to use it, but we get stuck in fear, then disobedience holds us back from operating in them. Gifts and calls come without repentance. We can easily become afraid of failure, thinking that we will be unsuccessful. On top of that, as God gives you the power to use your gift, the enemy is trying to denounce that the gifts are not real. You must stand on His promise and believe it.

Above all else, you have to be willing to operate in your gift. Know that your gifts work in different ways. A person could be in the need of healing in the spirit, and not their flesh. When you need healing in your spirit, you don't really see the manifestation in it. When there's evidence of healing in the natural, you see it in the natural. The spirit of fear is not of God. The enemy can cause you to be so fearful that the spirit of unbelief will creep in, and the spirit of doubt will overtake you. Now you're operating under the power and the authority of God, but you still have the spirit of the enemy that is manifesting in you too. God said that if you believe, then don't doubt him at the same time. To me, that's the epitome of being double minded, and hustling backwards.

Often times, we do not want to believe until after we have seen it, and that is what's really backwards. God wants you to believe and know that His miracles have already happened before you even received them. How do you expect miracles to happen, and you don't believe in the supernatural? If you only believe in the natural things, you'll never understand the Heavenly things. The issue in this day and time is that we lack the wisdom on how to teach each other on how to operate in our gifts. Many times, we don't even have evidence of our own gifts. It's very hard to try to teach someone something when you have no evidence and no knowledge of it yourself. Lack of belief makes it even worse. Even though you possess these amazing gifts, the enemy doesn't want you to believe. He doesn't want you to think that these things can happen.

We, as people, have been in this place of "show me, God, that you're real; give me some substance and you have to show me some real evidence that you do exist." When you want God to expose His works to you, speak to Him and talk to Him as if you would talk to anyone else in the natural, saying "Lord, I want you to reveal these things to me. I want you to show me how to operate under the unction. I want you to be able to give me the spirit of discernment." You must desire these things from the depths of your heart. You can't just speak anything out of your mouth. People will speak things, and not really believe it in their hears, and wonder why things do not come to pass.

Saints, as believers, every one of us are entitled to spiritual gifts. When these gifts started to manifest in my life, a lot of people thought it was not real. God gave me the gift of healing, and it was not until He started to use me for His purpose by healing the sick around me that people started to actually acknowledge my gift. You must believe in what you are praying for without any doubt. I command right now in the name of Jesus that the spirit of doubt will come out of the heart that is praying for healing. It is my prayer for you today that God will fill you with these gifts, and He will bring you into the light of His understanding.

## Fruits of the Spirit

Fruits of the Spirit are different from spiritual gifts, and they definitely have different functions on our journey. Fruits of the spirit demonstrate how we have grown in our walk with the Lord; it is a sign of spiritual maturity. They are attributes in which we are expected to have through the help of the Holy Spirit. In total, there are nine fruits of the Spirit, and these nine are a single entity that a believer is given together. These Godly attributes and virtues are: Love, Joy, Peace, Patience, Kindness, Goodness, Faithfulness, Gentleness and Self Control. They all help us as believers to live our lives the way God wants us to live, and it helps us be the light to unbelievers in a dark world.

I believe that you can relate with it when people expect you to behave differently from other people because you are a Christian, simply because the Fruits of the Spirit separates us from others. If you have the spirit of God inside you, it would be dishonoring if you still engage in worldly affairs. The Holy Spirit comes with these fruits that distinguishes us, and blesses us too!

## Evidence of a New Life

Once you surrender your life to Christ, you become a new creature; the Bible says, "Old things pass away and everything becomes new" (2 Corinthians 5:17). When the Holy Spirit dwells in us, the Holy Spirit does not just dwell in your heart, but also in your temple. Your whole body, at the point of confession and acceptance becomes the temple of Christ. During that stage, you live not as you used to live, but as a new being reborn into Christ. However, you cannot out of free will shed the old sinful nature and embrace the new nature of God. It is the Holy Spirit that will step in to help you as a new believer to take on a new nature; He comes with the evidence of a new life. Without the help of the Holy spirit, it is impossible to remove your bad nature and replace it with a good one. Through Christ Jesus, He strengthens us.

## Great Understanding of the Scriptures

When the Holy Spirit indwells in us, He teaches us all things. After we've experienced the indwelling of the Holy Spirit, we gain a better understanding of all things including the scriptures. The scripture will be new to you every day, as the Holy Spirit reveals new perspective, and can be understood on a daily basis. Treat your bible study just as a prescription order. As you experience challenges, and life lessons, ask yourself "What does the bible say about _____ (finances, depression, love, forgiveness etc?" Open your bible and seek the answer. (The Bible Concordance and even Google have made the search more convenient; thanks to our digital world...We have NO EXCUSES). Meditate on it throughout the day. This will help you with your daily living, and relationship with people. As it has been said, the world of God is a daily guide for us, and it is eternally relevant in our day to day activities. With the help of the Holy Spirit, we can be able to have a better understanding of the Bible and consequently our lives.

## Confirmation of Sonship

The indwelling of the Holy Spirit confirms that you are of the Lord, and that you have become an heir of God and a fellow-heir of Christ himself. For everyone who accepts and believes Jesus, they will be regarded as heirs to the throne.

Prayer is an important aspect of the Christian journey; it is through prayer that we get to connect with God, our father. Prayer helps us speak to God as we would our Father. God wants us to have a connection with Him, and

He wants to us see Him as someone we can turn to for anything. Being that we are joint-heirs with Christ, God wants to live amazing lives, granting us a free and unrestricted access to His presence.

One important work that the Holy Spirit does that we haven't yet mentioned is the work of an intercessor. The Holy Spirit does not only indwell us, he does not only teach and help us, he also intercedes on our behalf. In Romans 8:26, Apostle Paul talks about the spirit intercedes on our behalf with groaning which cannot be uttered. As humans, we don't always know how to pray; the spirit prays for us, and also teaches us what we should pray about whenever we pray. There is much power is prayer!

# CHAPTER 2

## Before the Power

*"God Doesn't Call the Qualified, God Qualifies the Called!"*

The power of God is available to all whom believes to use for the advancement of the Kingdom. God gives His power to every willing vessel who surrenders him or herself to the use of the Holy Spirit. Sometimes, the Lord chooses people and uses us even if we do not yet see how important we would be to do His will. Our Father does not call only those who are qualified; He equips whoever He calls with the right power and abilities to carry out the task that He has given unto them.

If you look in the bible, study the characters that were really unworthy; the ones that really lived a reckless life, and the ones that were really terrible were who God called to do great things. Paul the Apostle was a great example. He was a Christian murderer. When God blinded him, and opened his eyes to his true walk and his divine purpose, it was a reminder that no matter what you've done in life, God can make you a redeemer. If you know that you have never killed anyone in the natural, and this man killed people in the natural, and was used in a great and mighty way, compare yourself and God using you for your greater good. If he can be used, anybody can be used.

Changing your life right now is greater than changing your life later. If I knew then what I know now, I would have done it much earlier. In my past, the life I was living was very out of control, and reckless. I was doing everything under the sun from selling drugs, to being a whore monger, and doing many things that I wasn't proud of. Even in the midst of doing those things, I still knew that I had a calling over my life. Sadly, this knowledge did not stop me from living dangerously. The more that I did, the more convicted that I felt in my spirit. Looking back, I can truly say that I can identify with the Apostle Paul. There are many people who know of my past experiences, and the life that I used to live, and still look at me with disbelief. Regardless of if people choose to continue to condemn me for the shortcomings of my past, or see me for the man that I have been called to be, one thing is for certain: there is no denying the power of God moving through me. He has done a miraculous thing in my life. I am not perfect. I may have problems just like everyone else has, I have issues as well, but I have access to God just as everyone does. It is up to you to grow tired of living your way, and dedicate your life to living God's way. You can only run but for so long. The pivotal moment in my life was when I encountered my out of body experience that really made me change. Although God had been revealing His power to me, I was still running. Sooner or later, my running slowed down, and finally came to a complete stop. It took me over 40 years of wondering in the wilderness, but thank the Lord that I finally stopped running. These days, my running is for the Lord. I'm running to tell people about his goodness, and to tell them that there is power in the blood of Jesus. You see, the Heavenly Father does not reveal his miracles to you in order to keep them to yourself. He gives you testimonies for you to share so that someone else can be delivered and set free. In this world, there is someone uniquely designed and assigned to you. I truly feel that God chose me for a greater purpose, and I now realize that I am here to be a living sacrifice, and ultimately show you how to tap into the supernatural and receive your God-Given blessings. I am honored that God is using me to reveal his power. It's a blessing that he sees me worthy enough, and trusts that I would use his power correctly.

*When you learn to completely surrender to My perfect will and embrace the calling I have for you regardless of how difficult it gets, that's where my will can be truly done.*

If you are running from your gift, calling or blessing: Take Heed. God will put you in a place where you can't get out on your own. The spirit of conviction is evidence that He is moving down on the inside of you. Stop reopening doors that have closed. It's time to open up new doors. When the spirit of conviction moves through you, it's trying to convict you of the things that you are doing, knowing that what you were doing was wrong. What the Lord is saying is that even in your mess, he still has his hands on you. Even in those days where you might have been engaging in risky behaviors, God still had his hands upon your life. There is still a purpose for you here on this Earth. Despite it all, he knows that you are going to fulfill the purpose that he has designed for you. You can run, but you definitely cannot hide in the eyes of the Almighty! Many times people know that they are called by Him, but they try to disqualify themselves. Not knowing that they are actually building up a greater testimony to be used in the Kingdom. The more you run, it's more likely that you're going to continue to experience basic training, enduring a series of tests, repeatedly if necessary. Once you're done with basic training, you will be SHARP, DESIGNED, PERFECTED. The way God has orchestrated you to be. You have to go through it to get to it. There is a price to salvation, and it is necessary. Trust the process!

God gives out His power according to each person's abilities. Some people get the power of God and use it to the glory of His name, while others use it to the glorification of themselves. Whenever we use the gift in which God has given us, we are going to give account to God eventually. Matthew 25:14 explains that we see the story of a man who gave his workers talents according to their individual abilities and how fruitfulness and unfruitfulness was rewarded. God expects us as his children to bear fruits, and bring souls into his kingdom through the power and talent he has given us. When we refuse to bear fruits, we will face the consequences – if we also bear good fruits, we will be rewarded bountifully.

## Many Distractions

When the Lord has marked you to be used for a glorious purpose, the enemy will stand against this while attempting to derail the plan of God over your life. The devil knows that if a believer succeeds, then it becomes a great threat to his kingdom – which he never wants. One way that He attempts to sway us from the course is through the use of distractions. The devil adopts various means of distractions, and most of the time it works. Jesus in his teaching emphasized severely the need for people to cast every other thing away if they desire to follow him:

*Then he said to another, "Follow me." But he said, "Lord, let me first go and bury my father." Jesus said to him, "Let the dead bury their own dead, but you go and preach the kingdom of God." And another also said, "Lord, I will follow You, but let me first go and bid them farewell who are at my house." But Jesus said to him, "No one, having put his hand to the plow, and looking back, is fit for the kingdom of God."* Luke 9: 59-62

The excuses given by the two people in the passage above discusses family matters; one wants to bury his father, while the other wants to bid them farewell at his home before following Christ. The number one distraction we have to battle is the distraction from our families. If we are to truly walk with the Lord, we must be able to put the things of the Kingdom first. Although home is your first ministry, understand that initially the walk with Christ will be yours alone, as it is not one to be taken with your family or your friends. Although you are not hiding, isolation and the need to be hidden during your season will be very necessary. The walk with Christ is a decision between your light and darkness, between your own salvation and damnation; if your family or your friends have chosen to walk the broad way that leads to destruction, you cannot follow them down that path. Also, when the gift of the Divine starts to manifest in your life, the first group of people that may scorn you, or try to kill that gift could very well be the closest ones to you.

Over the course of my career as a preacher, I have been scorned and mocked by some family and friends who believed I did not know what I was doing. They judged me from my past, without looking at how I had been transformed inside and out. When God first showed his plans for my life, I told a few people about the power which God had given me, but they shut me down, and doubted me on the spot. In all essence, it did not matter whether they believed me or not; the power that God has given me cannot be taken away. No matter how sure you are about the call of God on your life, it is a conviction you have to see through alone; not with the help of family or friends. Just remember, everyone is not assigned to your calling, and that is okay too. Even still, sometimes people will put you in a place in their lives just to fill the spot, but not the position. Part-time kingdom advancement is not an option.

I must admit, this journey has not been easy. In fact, the closer you get to fulfilling God's promises, the lonelier the walk becomes. Overtime, I have learned to accept walking alone. Sometimes you can have people walking with you that are still against you. As long as I know I'm walking in the right direction, I know that the power of God walks with me. He said, I will never leave you, nor forsake you. The more you are alone, the closer you become with God. It's okay to have someone with you sometimes, but it is important to build intimacy with God, and know Him for yourself. You have to be very careful of who you allow to walk with you, because the same person who accompanies you could be trying to destroy you at the same time. That's where the spirit of discernment comes in. If at that point you feel that the same person that is walking with you is not really for you, it's time for you to walk a little faster. It's time for you to start walking into places where you know that they're not going to walk in. A true believer of Christ will follow you to the ends of the Earth. They have just as much faith as you have. Personally, I've experienced circumstances where people will say "Come on, come on, touch me, touch me, heal me, heal me, heal me". My discernment revealed that they have the spirit of rejection. I already know that they have the spirit of disbelief, and therefore can recognize when I am up against the spirit of rejection.

If you want to really work for the Almighty, you have to carry your cross and follow him, even if every other person around you is not willing to do the same. Jesus told anyone willing to follow him to carry his or her cross and follow him; it is a personal decision that everyone has to make. Even though the walk with Christ can be a lonely one, we are never alone; the power of God is always with us. This is something I have come to learn and understand; I am walking alone, but I am never alone. I do not find comfortability in thinking I always have individuals around me; when people find comfortability in having people around them, sooner or later those people will be taken away.

We need to develop to the stage that we can be in the presence of God alone. The truth is the more company we lose, the closer we get to God; when we surround ourselves with different types of friends and acquaintances, we are on path of being swayed away from His presence. Sometimes we make people, and even things our idols by investing more time in them than God, and we already know that God is not to be mocked. There's an African proverb I think about often; it says that a sheep that makes dogs its acquaintances will one day do things forbidden for sheep. This proverb explains the kind of affect acquaintances can bring into a believer's life. In your life, ask yourself this important question: Am I walking with sheep or dogs? If your answer is that you are walking with dogs, then you need to be mindful of the company you keep. You are a representation of the 3 people that you are around the most in your day to day affairs. Now, don't get me wrong, friends work in both positive and negative ways, but friends that will bring a negative affect should be avoided.

When the Bible says you should remove your eyes if it will lead you into sin, it was not only talking about our physical eyes or physical hands or legs. It talks about those people around us that may lead us astray also. As much as we need to drop bad influences, we also need to embrace similar minds; those who will lift us when we are weak. The Bible encourages us not neglect the gathering of the saints. We were created to be interdependent on one another. Find you some kingdom focused prayer warriors who will fight the good fight by your side when that season comes.

When you begin to walk with people, and then they begin to go in other directions, they may not have your best interest with them spiritually, and they will hinder your growth. They may have been put in your life to walk with you for a reason; to distract you from the goal. Sometimes, people will walk out of your life not because you are not good enough, but because they are not good enough for where God is taking you next.

Another similar distraction which causes many strong believers to fall is their career, business or even ministry. It is good to have a focus, it is great to have purpose, and it is awesome to have a blossoming and well-rounded life – God wants us to. The problem however is when we put those things ahead of our walk with God. Whatever we do should be done to glorify Him; anything we do that limits our service in the kingdom of God does not glorify him. We should be able to balance both our Christian journey and our endeavors, not allowing one to affect the other. The Bible says we should seek first the kingdom of God, and every other thing will be added unto us.

Nothing, no matter how important, is more important than our service to God. Of what benefit will it be for us to gain the world and lose our soul? (Matthew 16:26) In fact, I think it is better for anyone to lose an endeavor than to lose their souls. Now don't get me wrong, this doesn't mean we should be lazy and unmotivated in our lives; Christ wants us to excel in all we do. It may be tough to combine a well-rounded life with an unwavering walk with God, however, with the help of the Holy Spirit, we can combine anything and come out victorious. Put God first in all things and watch him change the trajectory of your life!

## Assassination (Matthew 2:16)

Often times, people want to hear what is good for them, they do not want to hear the truth. When Jesus came to the world, despite the fact that he could heal the sick and wake the dead, people still hated him because he told them the truth about themselves. We should never be afraid of saying the truth for whatever reason, because Jesus was never afraid. He stood his ground and spoke from the heart.

When King Herod heard about the birth of Jesus, he felt threatened and ordered that all male infants be put to death. Even though Jesus was just a new born, Herod ordered the assassination of a whole generation, because he did not want Jesus to reach his potential. As believers and as speakers of the truth, the world will never be satisfied if we reach our full potentials, so they will definitely seek to assassinate us as they did Christ; we should know that our existence is a huge threat to the kingdom of Satan. Unlike it was the case with Christ where Herod wanted to carry out a physical assassination on him, the kind of assassination believers are susceptible to is not physical, but spiritual and mental assassination.

Today, enemies of the gospel try to keep us from achieving the task God has given us through any means necessary. Look at the ways of the world today, and you will see oppression in its greatest form. God has given every one of us specific tasks even before we were born, but people will try to keep us from achieving success with this. It is imperative for us to be aware and conscious of the devices of the devil.

When the brothers of Joseph saw what he had been ordained to be by God, they got jealous and decided to plot against him. He was sold into slavery, and was made to suffer, merely for the fact that he had a bright future (Joseph's story and how his brothers sold him can be found in the whole of Genesis Chapter 37). Satan can and will try to use anyone against you to knock you off course. The most important thing we can do is to be vigilant and be watchful.

Peter, in one of his letters warned us to be vigilant always. He says, "Be sober, be vigilant; because your adversary, the devil walks about like a roaring lion, seeking whom he may devour" (1 Peter 5:8). The Bible also tells us that our warfare is not of the physical (2 Corinthians 10:4), all these point to the need for us to be armored for warfare. We must be prayerful, and to always seek the face of God. We as believers have no other alternative to prayer, even the bible tells us to "pray without ceasing". We need to be prepared for when we encounter spiritual warfare, and demonic forces in our day to day lives. They do exist. If we believe in heaven, surely we must understand and acknowledge that there is a hell too. Every supernatural encounter that I teach on is divinely first-hand, and not from man. I would like to share a demonic experience that allowed me to operate in my divine power.

## Casting Out Demons in the Nursing Home

As I traveled with my good friend Teresa, and two other ladies to the local nursing home, we began to go room to room and pray for the residents. One of the women asked a man if she could pray for him. He agreed, and once it was over, he looked at her with a smirk on his face, insinuating that her praying did nothing at all for him. I was quietly standing at the foot of his bed but noticed that he could not look at me. He would look at me, and then quickly look away. At that moment, the Lord spoke to me and said: "Now you pray for him." Obediently, I asked the man for permission to pray for him, and he also agreed. I began praying for him, and while doing so, I grabbed the bottom of his feet. Immediately, he began growling. When I opened my eyes, I could see that he was wrestling with a demon. All of a sudden, he let out a huge breath, and started to deflate like a balloon. I couldn't believe my eyes! The women accompanying me in the room began screaming, and I urged one of them to hurry and open up the window. As we were standing there watching the man deflate, I noticed that he was getting smaller. Then the Lord spoke to me and told me to explain to him that the spirit of unforgiveness was what he had been wrestling with. For years, the man was still holding on to the anger against someone he knew, which caused him great inner turmoil, and even affected his health. He had been in the nursing home due to undergoing a massive stroke. After he deflated like a balloon, the man began moving activities of his limbs. If I'm not mistaken, he is now out of the nursing home, and walking around regularly. Now, that's evidence of healing. At that moment, I truly learned that unforgiveness can keep you attached to those who have caused great pain. We have to free ourselves and forgive. By His stripes, we all are healed!

Pictured here is my friend Teresa, and witness to
the casting of the demonic spirit, she was a witness
of the Power of God!

## False Hope

Jesus is the same today, tomorrow and forever more. When we have started to grow steadily in the faith, and God has started to give us His power to use, Satan will come with false hope and lies, just to sway us from the ultimate prize. We should never forget that the only task of the devil is to distract us – as we have earlier established – we must never give him the chance to succeed at this. The devil is a liar, and the master of all deceivers. He constantly tries to poison our minds, telling us things that are untrue about ourselves, and those around us. Being the con man that he is, he tries to paint a deceitful picture for people, making outright lies seem like the truth. When he gives us a false perception of reality, he makes it appear so real that we think it is real. It takes the Spirit of God and a discerning Spirit to be able to tell the difference. Again, we must always be watchful and vigilant to be able to resist the devil's antics.

## How Satan Paralyzes Our Minds

We as humans think with a mind full of limited beliefs, but with the mind of Christ, there is no limit or boundaries of levels of our thinking, and when you think in the natural, there is only a limit to what you are able to think. Now, that is not to say that we are superhuman beings, or above God in any way. That's why only on T.V. there are superheroes, and even then, they are not so "super", because they all have some form of weakness. Superheroes do nothing but admire images of the devil's thinking that was above all, including God. Remember, with this thinking, Satan and his Angels were kicked out of Heaven because of this very thing. When you begin to think of yourself as super and above anyone, just know that you too have a weakness.

Many times, we want to do things according to our own purpose and hidden agendas. Understand that everything works and operates under the authority of God's will. Nothing happens unless God gives you permission. Yes, He gives you the authority, but you still have to get permission to use His authority. When there's a situation where someone needs to be healed, you must first ask God for permission to heal that person. It is important to realize that people may be put in a position where God doesn't want them to be healed in that particular way. Therefore, you must seek God for permission to do His will. Everything works and operates under the will of God. It does not work and is not being operated under your will. When we begin to operate in our own will, we are out of order. In the instance of coming under our own authority, we attempt to lay hands on people, and wonder why they are not being healed, and not being set free, making God look as if He really doesn't have the power.

We have all been exposed to limited beliefs since the day we were born. During our upbringings, we were taught certain pathologies, and thought processes that follow us into adulthood. When you are being reared up from being a young child, certain beliefs were deeply planted in your mind. Take yourself back to your childhood when you used to dream and had fearless faith. Look back at the history of your parents as well. Renounce any generational family iniquities, and curses that may have been passed down. Often times, we're fighting demons that our parents and grandparents should've fought and conquered. We must fight to get set free from generational strongholds and gain more control over the way we think, so that we can operate in order.

## Passion, Grace, and Love

Lastly, pray for forgiveness, and cast down bitterness, and resentment that we consciously or subconsciously may have been holding on to over the years. This is the area that usually causes us to continue to be stuck. Some people can't make it to tomorrow, because they cannot forgive themselves for what they did yesterday enough to embrace today. I challenge you to dig up the entire root, so that you can get on to healing and deliverance. Uproot everything that was planted inside of you that was not of God. Allow the Holy Spirit to renew your heart, and mind at the same time. Open your heart back up again. Your heart is the operation of your whole entire body. It can live without you, but you cannot live without it. When we express ourselves, what we desire should come from the heart, and not the mind. Whereas your mind will try to tell your body what to do, allow your heart to tell your mind what to do. Your heart can overrule your mind, but your mind tries to tell your mouth to speak certain things. The enemy easily desires through the mind, and tries to create conflict. Don't give in to the trick of the enemy. If you listen to your heart, you won't do what is wrong. Work diligently to be set free, indeed. Our freedom is not for us, it's a ripple effect that will go down for others. It doesn't matter what it takes to reach those who are lost, as long as you reach them. Embrace your journey; what you went through was never about you, it's about who you are called to. Catch that!

## The Hand of God: Glory Cloud

As a guest at my Sister's home, I was lying in my niece's bed praying and meditating before going to sleep. All of a sudden, a cloud came in the room and hovered over top of my bed. It instantly turned into the shape of a hand. As I lay there is disbelief, I was careful not to make any sudden movement. Not wanting to startle the whole house, I quietly laid there watching it's every move. It came down towards me, and its index finger touched my forehead. When that happened, I saw a dark presence leave my body. I jumped up in the middle of the floor, and said "Lord, what in the world was that?". I began crying but did not get an immediate answer from God. I was determined to find out though. For three days, I constantly begged God to reveal to me what happened to me that night. On the third night, the Lord woke me up around 3 am, and He said that was the spirit of anger that had been trying to destroy me for 40 years. At that moment, that same spirit of anger tried to enter back into my body, but I recognized what it was, and I didn't open up to it. The bible says that once an unclean spirit leaves your body, it will try to seek rest, and it will try another place of rest to go. In other words, it would try to find another willing vessel to live in. If it cannot find rest, then it will try to return from which it has come from. The bible says, if it comes back into you, it brings seven times more demons with it. We have to resist evil at all costs. The devil has more faith in your weaknesses than you can even imagine. The anecdote to break the cycle is love, not hate.

Listen to your heart. Trust your heart. When you begin to trust your heart, you will soon see that your heart will not lead you wrong, but your mind will. Our heart is what makes us believers of the power of God. It will allow us to feel the true and living power. When faced with a conflict, instead of immediately reacting, quiet your mind, and listen with your heart. Instead of coming to God after the damage has been done, consult with God first. Exercise having a sound mind, and do not give in to the temptations of the enemy. Just as when Satan took Jesus off, and he tempted him saying "If I give you all of this, the world, will you bow down and worship me?" You cannot allow temptations, lust, and pictures in your mind to overtake you. Cast it down immediately! Every single day, we have to intentionally cast down strongholds from our minds. You have to listen with your heart.

Let me tell you about the word, "heart". The word "heart" is spelled h-e-a-r-t. The word of God says, "If he has an ear, let him hear", therefore you must listen with the ear that's in your heart. The first two letters in heart is "h-e", and if you look at the other letters, "e-a-r", take the "h" out and you see "ear". Then you put the "h" back on and you see "hear". H-E-A-R. That is what the spirit of the Lord is saying.... Just some food for thought for you, as you go about your daily life. Free your mind, and your heart will follow!

# CHAPTER 3

# Blurry Visions (Mark 8:24)

## Small Spiritual Appetite

God's expectation for every believer is that we are not to remain as ignorant and naive Christians for life; we are expected to grow and reach maturity. While we do not always expect our children to become independent the moment they start growing, but as they grow, we expect them to drop some habits which are proportionate to their age. If someone accepts Christ today, they are expected to have some level of immaturity, however at some point they are expected to grow and mature. We are God's investments, when we grow and become fruitful, we become assets; when we remain stagnant, we become liabilities. None of us should strive to be a liability for God, we are expected grow and bear fruits.

In order to grow as believers, we need to first surrender to the Holy Spirit, and allow Him to direct our spiritual life, teaching us what we do not yet know. We truly need the Holy Spirit for a new, and unique perspective. It is one of the tasks of the Holy Spirit to interpret things for us and make known things that are hidden.

Even though we shouldn't waste time being stagnant, we also shouldn't be in such a hurry to achieve full maturity when we are in our early stages. Take things day by day, and give yourself the same level of self compassion, and grace as our Heavenly Father gives us. It is important that we allow the Holy Spirit to take full control and lead us every step of the way. Taking baby steps and moving up gradually through development and to maturity is very important for us while we transition. This process will allow us soak in every experience that God wants us to have, and make them useful for our life on a daily basis. The word of God is best taken in once at a time, allowing the Holy Spirit to interpret things into our minds.

As a true believer, your personal mission should be to become completely humble, then silent with a keen ear. A lot of times when we begin to share with people that God has endowed us with certain types of gifts, the spirit of betrayal, the spirit of hatred, and the spirit of jealousy will come upon others to try to distort and contaminate what God has revealed to us. Next, continue to stay in a place of obedience. This will ensure that you do not act out of order, abusing your authority to be a healer.

I can personally recall that although there have been times where those who have a spirit of rejection and disbelief would try to challenge me, I had to remain diligent in knowing that if God said it, then it is so. Lastly, you must maintain a spirit of discernment. The spirit of discernment is truly what will keep you spiritually aligned when dealing with people. Once you tune in and tap into this, intentions will be revealed, and you will begin to see different types of spirits that are within your loved ones. It could be within your mother, your father, even your friends. You can see how they're operating in the spirit, and because you see them for who they are, this gives you a silent opportunity to decide how you choose to proceed with them.

It is in our secret closet that we can pray for people and be mindful that not everyone is assigned to you. Do your part and leave the rest up to God. Plenty of newly formed believers in the faith today want to jump from being an immature Christian to a fully grown, and fully matured Christian overnight. God does not like to jump protocol. He likes it when we follow the long and tiring staircase; this way we can learn important lessons about how to tough out the journey, and ultimately give Him the highest praise for the blessings, and lessons.

## My Vision

I said "LORD, I'm ready to do what you called me to do", and He said to me "sit down". Look inside the word SIT DOWN. There's a hidden message. I had to visualize the word SIT DOWN. The first thing He revealed was that I want to see if you can hear me. Two, will you follow my instructions? Three, will you obey me? He said to me: "Yes you have the gift of healing, and yes I've shown you signs of wonders, but what good will you be on the battlefield with the proper equipment and not know how to use it?"

*And it shall come to pass in the last days, said God; I will pour out of my Spirit upon all flesh: and your sons and your daughters shall prophesy, and your young men shall see visions, and your old men shall dream dreams. Acts 2:17*

## Busy Doing Nothing

*"When you realize that this is not about you or your ministry but about Me and My ministry"* …

Nowadays, it's easy to be busy being engaged in church and kingdom activities, just keep in mind that we still need to preserve our energy towards the effective expansion of God's kingdom. Engaging in too many things at once in the church without living a holy life or following the footprints of Jesus is an attempt to bribe God. Don't be one way on Sunday and be a completely different person throughout the rest of the week. Attempting to bribe God with activities is an attempt to deceive and mock God; God is not to be deceived, neither should He be mocked.

While it is easy to deceive man, with activities bringing in a lot of accolades, awards even, from the church, God looks deep into our hearths and sees the sin. Remember when Samuel was asked to go and ordain David? Samuel got there and saw all the big, hefty brothers that David had, he was sure it must be among them. However, God chose the smallest of all to be anointed as the next king of Israel (1 Samuel chapter 16). God could care less what we do for him if our hearts and soul are not pure and free of just because we want to be seen. God wants us to work for Him, because we believe in the kingdom mandate, not because we want to be seen. Doing God's work with the mindset of being seen or being noticed is eye service. Don't get caught up in the Peacock Spirit of "look at me, look at me". God is omnipotent, and He sees all; He knows our deepest and our innermost thoughts. Consequently, He knows when our service to Him is merely a case of eye service. It is unfortunate today that a lot of the people that work in the kingdom of God do it for financial and physical gains, not for the love of the gospel.

For anyone who does not accept Christ, their soul is damned, that we all know. However, the same fate awaits those who serve God with the half of their hearts. It will be unfortunate for someone who believes they have been working for God to find themselves in hell. Half service is no service at all, anyone who falls in this category is busy doing nothing. How do you know you fall into this category? You fall into this category if your heart is not clean, and you do things for personal gratification.

One of the church's greatest problems is that we have been operating out of order while kingdom building, sometimes out of selfishness. Because of this disobedience, many of us tend to be lost, stuck in bondage, and will continue to be confused with a contaminated spirit, causing us to lose faith. In my opinion, a key issue is that everyone is trying to be in position, operating in the same office, and no one really wants to play their true, divine part. Everybody wants to be the head, but no one wants to be the server. When God has called you divinely, you are a server. You are not to sit back, and let the people serve you; you're supposed to really be serving your people. There are too many who operate in a position that God has not called them to be in, causing great chaos. For this very reason, there is a spiritual war going on inside of the church world. Every day, I see preachers against pastors, fighting for position. It's causing a lot of confusion in the church. Meanwhile, our congregation is suffering in deep bondage and spiritual warfare, lacking the knowledge, wisdom and understanding on how to take authority and power through God.

So many of you continue to stay in bondage, simply because you do not know another way out. Not only are you in bondage, but you have the spirit of fear that has been planted on the inside of you. Some of us have allowed the spirit of religion to run our lives and kill our efforts to live out a righteous life. Be careful with who you allow to feed you spiritually. What happens is that after unqualified leaders that are not divinely called by God begin feeding you spiritually, they begin feeding you things that cause you to only look to them for help. They are teaching and training you in a way that keeps you crippled, and dependent on them, and not on God. This could lead into an ungodly soul tie. You simply cannot afford to allow any, and everyone feed you. Every day I see folks allowing modern day organized religion to brainwash them into thinking that they cannot operate in life without their leaders. This dysfunction is codependency at its best. No one should have so much power or authority to even do that. That's just like when Pharaoh had the people in bondage, and God sent Moses to tell Pharaoh to let my people go. They are God's people. That's the problem. Man has taken the power into his own hands, and he has taken God's people, making them his people.

For these reasons, younger generations are looking for new things to fulfill them spiritually. I don't necessarily feel that they all are lost either. They want a real, authentic relationship with Christ, connections, true intimacy, and acceptance. We must all come together to bridge the gap of this disconnect. Our young people are smarter than we give them credit, and are no longer going to stand for the foolishness of the dysfunction in today's church. They seek the unwavering truth, and I strongly feel that somehow, we have lost our way. It starts with owning the fact that we are meant to be interdependent with each other, not independent, and definitely not codependent. This cannot be a one man show; we have to be willing to serve one another. God intended us to all come together on one accord and represent the body of Christ. Let's get back in alignment, go to our Heavenly Father to repent for our selfish ways, and get back into His Divine Order. This time around, doing it all His way, and not our own.

## Focused on Heaven, Miserable on Earth

Unbeknownst to many of us, some of us in the name of being heaven-conscious lead a miserable life. My dear brothers, and sisters, realize that you are royalty. Get out of the habit of disqualifying yourselves and take your rightful seats at the table. The day you truly realize this, your life will be forever changed. You see, we are in the world, but we are not of the world; this is an eternal truth. The fact that we are not of the world does not mean we cannot excel in the world. We are the head and not the tail. (Deuteronomy 28:13); if the Bible validates this truth, why should we then reduce our lives to misery? We are expected to lead anywhere we may be, even as we pass through the face of the earth, we are expected to lead and leave a footprint. We are expected to be conscious of heaven, but we should never forget to spread the goodness of God on earth by making our lives a blessing to others.

On another note, some of us are so focused on heaven that we are of no good to anyone on earth. A Christian that is of no good on earth cannot bear any fruit for God. Some of us want to see the power of God at work before we can accept a message of good news. If you nourish your spiritual body alone, and abandon your physical body, your whole life will not be an example of the goodness of God. Our lives should be one that unbelievers would love to emulate, not one that would doubt God's healing power. Take good care of yourself in mind, body, and soul. Love yourself holistically. A life can only be fruitful when our lives are healthy. Our Father loves us so much that He wants us be to be successful in all areas of life. When we possess a thriving, powerful image of ourselves in the eyes of others, unbelievers see the God in us, and that ultimately leads souls to Him. Rest knowing that in this life, you may be the only physical image of Jesus to the people who need to see Him the most. It is your job to represent a Christ centered life at all times.

# CHAPTER 4

# Transitioning

*"When I was a child, I spoke like a child, I understood as a child; but when I became man, I put away childish things."*

*(1 Corinthians 13:11)*

Have you ever seen anyone who grows old and refuses to die? It has been established that change is a constant thing, and most times, change is either growth itself or something happens in life that forces us to grow. I am certain everyone can relate with the idea of change, as everyone alive has had to deal with change at one point in life. Growth is generally a positive thing, and it is something we all look forward to seeing work out in our lives. When friends and family see something positive in us, they give us the remark that we are growing. Our response to this kind of remark would be to smile, knowing they have just noticed a good development in us. Growth is something we should always proud of, something we always like people to notice in us.

God wants us to grow and develop into transformed Christians. Just know that we cannot reach our full potential the very day we discover that we have potential; it takes time, patience and learning. As newfound believers, the Lord does not expect us to grow into full spiritual maturity the very day we accept Christ. He is a miracle worker, but God is not a magician; there is order and protocol even in spiritual affairs. In 1 Corinthians 13:11, Paul talks about the growth process for a believer; as a child, still growing in the spirit, we are expected to act and behave according to our level of spiritual understanding.

As we grow, we are expected abandon things that we used to do, because we have acquired more knowledge of the Lord. Sometimes, we tend to get so passionate about the work of God and fail to give ourselves enough time to grow and mature. It is unfortunate that the overzealousness often gets replaced by frustration, and outright lack of interest in spiritual things, ultimately leading us to backslide altogether. It is important that you take your steps gradually, and give yourself the time, and space to grow.

If we have always lived a life of sin, we should not expect that the moment we give our life to Christ that the struggle between temptation is over immediately. Understand that giving our life to Christ also increases the number of attacks from the devil to make us lose our salvation. As being newly birthed, hold firmly to the Holy Spirit, and allow him to guide your every move. We need to give God some time to fix our sinful nature, and lustful desires, by replacing them with desires of the spirit.

Don't faint or get frustrated that the spiritual journey is not as fast you would have expected; most people expect to start speaking in tongues the very day they give their lives to Christ, and to start seeing visions the next day. When this does not happen, they feel like they are ineffective and of no use to God. Knowing that the journey on the path of righteousness is a lifelong process where we consistently have to grow in the spirit will help instill confidence in your decision to try Jesus.

I've come to realize that in our spiritual walk, we never really reach full maturity in the Lord, and we'll forever be a student. The walk with our Lord is a continuous process where we grow daily. It is imperative for those of us who have grown in the faith to mentor new believers and help them achieve a transition from their worldly nature into the body of Christ. Often, we see that they are judged for their previous lives, and they are made to feel like outcasts in the body of Christ. This is against the teachings of Jesus, and any believer that does this is not yet mature in the faith. It is not ours to judge, it is ours to correct and to encourage. God is the judge of all. Self compassion for others is a must. We all are on a journey, but there are no winners to the race.

God's way is to grow in the spirit through praying, studying the word, and fellowshipping with each other.

# CHAPTER 5

## Giving Up is Never an Option

How many times in our lives have we come across the phrase "giving up" when faced with challenges, and there seems to be no way out? One thing common to all of us is the propensity to give up when things begin to go south, causing us to hit rock bottom. It's natural for us to feel like giving up when the chips are down, but time has shown us again and again, people who refused to throw in the towel always triumph at the end.

We must never forget that we have not achieved anything if we stop midway. The journey with our Heavenly Father is a tough one, there are many stumbling blocks on the road that would seek to distract us; we must never allow them. Our focus should be on God, the author and the finisher of our faith. One of my favorite scriptures, which has taken me far throughout my years is: "I can do all things through Christ which strengthens me." Philippians 4:13. It tells us that whatever life throws our way, we must stay resilient. In Philippians 12:4, the Apostle Paul wrote "I know both how to be abased, and I know how to abound: everywhere and in all things, I am instructed both to be full and to be hungry, both to abound and to suffer need." What a great resilient spirit he had. How did he get to this level of resilience? Paul suffered greatly for the cause of Christ, and he held on until the very last time, not allowing persecutions to scare him away. The reason why many of us are afraid to walk with God is because we are afraid of persecution.

There could come a time in our lives when all we depend on fails us, including our knowledge, strength, resources and intellect. Hard times have driven so many to the edge of insanity, into depression, fear, hatred and anger and eventually suicide. Have you ever gotten to the point in life where you never considered giving up as an option no matter the obstacle? How do you develop a resilient spirit like that of the apostle Paul? What does a person need to do to continue in the faith no matter what? If we are able to depend on the Holy Spirit for strength, He will help us through.

We sometimes get to our low points in our lives when we may even ask the question if God is aware of all we are going through. We look back and begin to feel that all of our efforts are a waste of time. When the willpower to keep on moving seems to have been sucked out and you begin to think "where do I go from here?" When all things are falling apart, it is not the time give up, it is the time to look up unto

God. Sometimes He allows us to hit rock bottom, so that we can look up. He is the ROCK at the bottom!

## Trusting the Next Step

Our resilience, our strength just like that of Apostle Paul must be in God, through his words. Though the journey may be tough, we should have faith that with the help of the Holy Spirit, becoming victorious is non-negotiable. Trust in knowing that God will lead the way.

It is impossible to please the Almighty without faith in him, we must realize that we have to believe and stand on His words. Your faith in the word of God, gives you the ability to overcome the challenges life throws at you. The woman in Mark: 5, had never seen Jesus before, the bible reiterated this fact that she had only heard about Jesus but that was enough to spring up belief once again in her. In Mark 5:30, her faith so much pleased Jesus that he was forced to turn and look at her. This shows us how much our undoubted faith in God so much pleases Him, ultimately compelling him to give us what we need.

The Lord will give us the strength we need to overcome, if we only look up to Him for strength. This demonstrates our trust in him and also in his word. He wants us to trust him for our health, our careers, our finances, our families and even in whatever critical situation we might find ourselves. In order to demonstrate this kind of faith, you must believe that the word of God is true. This position makes you take a stand no matter what comes your way, and for you to not waver in your faith. You cannot demonstrate your faith in God if you do not believe his words are the truth, and foundation of belief. We must lean on the insight that is given us through the Holy Spirit.

## Don't Move

*Tell My people", the Spirit of the Lord told me, "that I see their labor for me, and nothing is in vain. Tell them that I see how tired they are getting and how some are crying out to me for relief. This is what I want them to know. Release this message."*

When it seems that all hope is lost, the scripture has made it known to us that God is always there for us and whatever he is planning is always going to be to our own good. We might not have in details what God's plan for us is, but we can be rest assured that they would work out for our good. God said He has planned it out. If He says He has then He has, you just have to believe Him and not perturbed by the circumstances around you. God will never give up on you, He is interested in taking care of you. Your life is full of countless possibilities, and there is so much yet to do, lives to be positively influenced, and too many dreams to fulfill to quit now. He has a wonderful plan and place for you, and your future holds great promise.

Holding on firmly to God's word gives you assurance that He would see you through is enough strength to become resilient. It is the kind of belief that can make you overcome any form of obstacle. You can have the God of the universe behind you, and still think of quitting. And if you have, it's not too late to snap out of wallowing in self-pity, and begin to walk in the light of the knowledge that no matter how terrible it may be, He has got it all planned out. The Lord already knew beforehand that the days of problems will come, but He has told us He will never abandon us, More often than not, we are the ones who abandoned Him when the chips were down. We stopped talking to Him, then the doubts came, we allowed fear to set in, we worried obsessively, then we allowed depression and anxiety all creep up on us. Instead, we should've been worshipping through it all, casting our cares upon Him.

God won't have us put all of our high hopes out there, only to fail us in the end. He said, "I know what I am doing". We have to be still and know. He will not call us into His kingdom and leave us hanging when we need him the most. Our Father loves us more than we love ourselves. If

He has called us to work for Him, He will see that we finish it successfully.

# CHAPTER 6

## The Building of Your Faith

Now that you believe and have faith in Christ, it doesn't all end there. There is a need to reassure ourselves of our faith in Him. We need to grow in our faith. Building up faith simply means to become one minded with the word of God until you get to that level where nothing moves you anymore. The building of your faith helps you as a believer to grow and toughen up; to become steadfast and be able to persevere when the going gets rough. It's just like an athlete going through his training routine. If your muscles aren't strong enough, no matter how good you are, you will not last long out there in the game when you become faced with opposition.

There is a place for preparation so that whatever the opposition you come against, you can withstand it. If you eat food regularly, it will build you up physically. But if you eat right and do not exercise, all you will do is get flabby and out of shape. In much of the same way, you need to feed your faith on God's word. You also need to exercise your faith, because if you do not, your faith muscles will be out of shape. Otherwise, you will not be able to do much spiritually when it comes to moving mountains in your life.

Building your faith means that you can feed your spirit on God's Word and thereby feed your faith, because God's Word is faith food. We also have to do our part and exercise our faith to develop it, allowing it to grow. The more knowledge you have, the more you are better equipped to be able to pass your examinations. That is why it is so important to be spiritually and emotionally mature. You have to be equipped with the right kind of knowledge to be able to answer the appropriate set of questions that God may ask you. Situations and circumstances throws us is in the word of God so that we can build and prepare ourselves for whatever challenge that might come before us. God will not do this for us, we must do it by ourselves.

## For Your Eyes Only

In building faith, sometimes God gives a vision that is just for you only. In other words, He gives you a vision to run with. When you have a God-given vision, and He is preparing you for a course, something about you changes. It's a time when God has a part, and you have a part in bringing your vision to reality. God partners with you so that your relationship with Him grows stronger during the process. A look into the Bible, gives us examples of men who had a vision, but had no idea on how to go about it or how to make such a vision become a reality. A big dream requires a strong belief. Someone said if a dream comes from God, it will be so big that you can't do it on your own. If you could do it effortlessly without breaking a sweat, you would not need faith. So, what is to be done when God gives us a vision to pursue? When God gives us a vision, He provides every resource needed to accomplish the vision. In your quest to fulfill your God given vision, you can be rest assured that God won't leave you all alone to sort it out all by yourself. You need to request His help and be attentive to the impressions and guidance of the Holy Spirit. I want to share with you one of my proudest moments that demonstrate a Father's Love, and how faith works:

## Cancer Free

One day I was at work, and my wife at the time, called me crying, saying that I needed to come home right away. Our 12-year-old daughter Demetria had been diagnosed with a rare form of cancer. On the way home, the Lord spoke to me in the car. He told me to get a pen, and paper and write down a healing prayer. I was to give it to my daughter when I arrived home. I spoke God's instructions to her, which was to touch the area that she was in pain, believe that she can be healed, and she'll be healed. That's all I did. We began receiving boxes of medicine to our house and visiting the doctor to learn more about the cancer she had. We were told that her hair was going to fall out, and she needed to have treatment and undergo the chemotherapy process. The morning that we took her to the hospital to start her therapy, the doctor indicated that he wanted to run one more test before she was given chemo. The doctors came back in the room dumbfounded saying that they could not give her any chemo because, whatever had been there is now gone. They ran test after test, and still could no longer find the cancer. She is 21 years old to this day and is cancer free. Cancer free! Hallelujah.

Pictured is my daughter Demetria, Cancer Free! Glory!!!

## Be Prepared for A Little Discomfort

When God begins to work with you to bring His vision for your life, He takes you to a level where you have not been before. That does not mean all the hard work has already been done, and that it is now time to relax. You cannot afford to become distracted or carried away by little successes on the way to accomplishing your vision. When Moses led the children of Israel out of Egypt, he suddenly realized he had become the leader of a nation. His status had suddenly changed from a fugitive who became a shepherd, to a national hero. What a tremendous overnight elevation! You would have thought it was time for Moses to relax and begin to enjoy the benefits that came with this great position, but the reverse is the case. When the army of Pharaoh pursued after the children of Israel, they turned to Moses for help. Some even questioned his intention on why he brought them out of the land of Egypt in the first place. Now that's not a position many would love to be in, but it was a situation in which Moses found himself.

You cannot get comfortable with where you are in God. Once elevation comes because of your God given vision, it brings a little discomfort. The discomfort is necessary for you to be able to make the necessary adjustments needed. It may require a whole shift in your priorities, plans and focus. It may even require you to part with something very dear to you. We can see that sometimes the discomfort that comes with elevation, is God's way of telling us we are not there yet.

## The Elevation is a Demonstration from God

In running with your God given vision for your life, you are bound to experience some changes. Changes in the way you think, the way you see things become different. Everything you do is always geared towards the actualization of your vision, which propels you to step up. Since you know your faith, and the power to actualize the vision comes from the Almighty, then you cannot afford to be far away from him. You want to draw closer to him more than ever before, and on a deeper level. In the Bible, Moses was always in constant communication with God, even then, he was before God, and was revealed his vision for his life. We must allow the elevation to take place. It tells us that we now have an assignment to pursue, and we must be ready to step up. Elevation might be God's way of telling you that He is moving you from one sphere of influence or authority to the other, and from one opportunity to the next.

Elevation is God's evidence to allow us to see that He is moving us forward in our destinies, causing us to advance in His purpose, preparing us for bigger assignments than we have ever known. In our desire to fulfill God's great purposes for our lives, the Lord begins to move in ways in our lives that will result in a change of focus and priority. Moses' priority changed from being a shepherd who only cared about feeding the flocks and taking care of his family, to one who had to lead a whole nation out of bondage. He became the leader of his country overnight. Through him, God performed many signs and wonders not only in the land of Egypt but also on the way to the Promised Land. It's like being elevated to the position of a boss in your job. Whenever God gives a vision he makes provision available for whoever is to run with the vision. Elevations are bound to come on the way, but it is not the time to become extravagant in thinking, but to remain grounded and allow it to take place the way God wants it.

## I Spoke to the Wind

Let me tell you about the wind. I was at work one day, and it was extremely windy. The wind was blowing so hard to the point that a huge flag on top of the building was literally slapping the top of the roof. At that moment, I prayed out "Ok Lord, not by my power, but by your power I command the flag to stop right now in the name of Jesus! Wind, I command you to stop blowing on that flag." Right then, the flag came to a complete stop, but the wind was still blowing. I then instructed the wind to release, and the flag started back blowing. You see, from time to time, I like to put in my spirit some of the things that God has done in the bible, and His promises. For example, it was amazing how He spoke to the wind, and it ceased, then the sea became at peace. If He has said that whoever believes in Him will do the works He has been doing, and will do even greater things than Him, then understand that it is embedded in your spirit, and you have the authority to speak it! Of course, He's not giving you the power to do more than Him, but He's giving you the authority to do more. Greatness awaits you, my friends!

# CHAPTER 7

## Challenging God at His Word

A confession of your faith means you are receiving the promises of God into your life, and He always keeps His promises. Faith is a confession of God's word, and when you take God at His Word, He honors His word. The Bible says in Psalms 138:2 that God honors His word more than His name. In the Bible, there are both acceptable and unacceptable ways of challenging the word of God. While with one challenge comes our knowledge of the word of God and it is acceptable, the other is rooted in doubt, and it is unacceptable.

The Bible talks about those who challenge God out of their doubtful minds. The Bible says, "For let not that man think that he shall receive anything of the Lord" (James 1:7). Challenging God at His word must solely be based on faith in God through His words, and not out of contempt or disrespect. God was angry with the children of Israel, because they challenged Him out of doubt. In spite of the various mighty things He did for them, their minds were still consumed in doubt. They approached God in a rude and ungrateful way; they willfully put God to the test by demanding the food they crave (Psalms 78:18). That is not how faith works. You can imagine how it would feel if a child you have always done everything for begins to doubt you and puts you to the test based on their doubt.

The Israelites were obviously in a situation where they needed God to intervene, but the point at which they tested Him, was when doubt and fear overtook them. They concluded that the Lord had abandoned them. They questioned His reliability, because they believed God was not meeting their expectations. Another part of the Bible explains this position in clearer terms. It says, "and they tempted God in their heart by asking of meat for their lust" (Psalms 78:18). The children of Israel where simply tempting God. The latter part of the verse made another point clear to us that the children of Israel asked of meat for their lust. As it has been established, it is good to challenge God at His words, but whenever challenging the word is done just to gratify our lustful desires, it is unacceptable in the sight of God.

The acceptable way of challenging the Almighty is through the demonstration of faith in obedience to His word. Holding on to the word of God and confessing it even when everything around us is saying the opposite is a great example. When our Father sees faith in His word in action, He is bound to honor is word. When challenges come your way, you go back to Him with confidence in the written word of God. He already knows when we challenge His word out of faith or out of doubt. He sees our hearts, and knows our intentions, and will uphold the honor of His word as long as we come from a heart of faith.

## Make Sure to Be sure

Our God-given vision comes through a revelation, and is not self-invented, we just happen to discover it. The Lord may decide to also drop it into our hearts in the form of ideas and concepts, just know that they are usually God given, and man driven. Include God in everything that you do. We cannot afford to leave God out of our plans. Leaving God out of our plans could be to our detriment. Making God a part of the plan is always healthy for our spiritual growth. It makes you want to know what plans are for you. In the process, you begin to develop a closer and personal relationship with him, because if you don't you will find it difficult to access whatever he has in store for you. This is also a period where you wait on God for his own will, and purpose to come to pass. As we continue to push on, God will begin to build patience in us through the tests of life. How many of us could use a little more patience?

When Jesus was teaching his disciples how to pray, He said, "thy will be done on earth as it is done in heaven". Jesus had a God given mission while He was on earth therefore, He had to pray for God's will to be done. Remember, the vision is not yours initially, it is God given but man driven.

Most of the strength we will need to be able to achieve our vision comes from the place of prayer. Prayer is the way through which we communicate our plans to God, seeking His guidance. It is a way of telling God about the choices we intend to make, seeking His opinion to know whether He approves or disapproves of it. In Jesus' earthly ministry, He was always in constant communication with God. He asserted this himself in John 5:19 when He said, "the son can do nothing of himself". He was simply saying, "as far as making some decision concerning the vision goes, it's not entirely up to me, because I still need to consult with God the Father". Jesus demonstrated time and time again by going quietly to the place of prayer.

*I had to constantly humble myself to My Father's perfect will and let His Spirit work. Why do you think was I going up to the mountain to spend time alone with My Father each day? I had to re-charge and let His Spirit move.*

In prayer, God readily gives us His divine wisdom if we ask Him. Since He is the source of wisdom for all things, we should know that He not only has the answer, He is the answer. The scripture says in Jeremiah 33:3, "call upon me, and I will answer you, and I will show you great and mighty things you do not know." Divine wisdom is not common sense; it is more than that. Divine wisdom brings divine directions. God will lead you along a path that will fulfill His plans for your life. He is the one who knows the direction you are to follow, and will lead accordingly. If you sense any anxiety or confusion, keep praying. God's wisdom will direct your paths in a peaceful manner.

Asking God for direction, is not being lazy, and does not imply being weak. It means that you are allowing Him to take charge. The Bible encourages us to do so. "Trust in the Lord with all your heart and lean not on your own understanding. In all your ways acknowledge Him, and He shall direct your path" Proverbs 13:5-6. Seeking God's direction is wisdom personified, and it demonstrates absolute dependence on God.

While much emphasis has been placed on seeking God's guidance, it is also important to note that obedience to God's given direction will save us a lot of pain. God would not force us to follow His directions; it is left for us to decide if we would follow Him or not. We can be rest assured that our own knowledge, wisdom, strength and intellect have their own limitations, and can fail us when we least expect them to. Don't ever think you can outsmart God by hijacking his plans. No sooner than later you would hit a roadblock, and you would be forced to turn back to Him. Merciful God He is, and He always accepts us back, but you would discover that precious time had already been wasted, which could all have been avoided if we had stuck with God in the first place.

## Building Up Your Appetite

"You will seek Me and find Me when you seek Me with all your heart" (Jeremiah 29:13). Our greatest privilege is to hunger after God and seek Him with all our heart. We must be willing to develop a deeper spiritual thirst, and hunger for the Lord. It is an active state that results in you seeking out the object of desire that will satisfy your need, the object of desire here being Him. Building up your spiritual appetite entails you longing to encounter the Almighty, to be with Him, and to be filled with His Spirit. To be in his Presence, and to do whatever it takes to get closer to Him. This often leads us into the place of intimacy, where we will experience not only the revelation He wants to give us, but we will also catch His heart.

When we hunger and thirst for God, we will seek Him, and when we seek Him, we will be filled and empowered. Our hunger is a measurement of our spiritual health. Here are some ways that we can build up our spiritual appetites, while staying in the word of God:

1. ***Read and apply the word of God.*** This is to have the desire or to long for the word of God, no matter how little the desire may be. It's a starting point for all of us. In addition to the desires, we should feed it. You can't just stop at having a desire, you must feed the appetite you do have, so that it will grow. To build up your appetite, make a deliberate effort, to set apart time to listen, read and study the word of God

2. ***Get Quiet and Seek Solitude.*** There are some things that try to compete with our desire for the word of God. They come in form of distractions, and there are lots of them around. They may look harmless in nature, but if

they could shift our focus and attention and, worse, destroy our appetite for Scripture, they definitely need to go. It's a sacrifice we have to make. Competing appetites could be in form of the excessive amounts of time spent on various social media platforms, excessive time spent in social engagements, and all other activities that don't contribute in anyway whatsoever to our spiritual growth. Distractions can also come when you try to fill the space God ought to occupy in your life with salary, status, success, passion, possessions, power, prestige, or anything other than God, it's not going to be fulfilling.

3. *Associate with people of like passion.* The desire and yearning to build up your appetite could be contagious. Be surrounded by people who thirst, and hunger after God and righteousness, or people who are further on in the journey than you. Read and study books of anointed ministers, and people who inspire you. You can even listen to their messages and podcasts. Join the assembly of God's people, and fellowship together with them. The people that you spend most of your time with have an influence on what you do. If you hang out with people who only care about politics or sports, that's mostly what you're going to care about too. Don't get me wrong

thinking that discussing sports and politics are not bad, but they shouldn't take the place of your time with God. The word of God should always be first on the list and knowing more of God should be the number one goal.

4. ***Practice Self-Discipline.*** The place of spiritual discipline cannot be overemphasized. It is one of the bedrocks of spiritual growth. To study for an exam takes discipline even if you don't feel like it, or when other things are calling for your attention. Building up your appetite also requires some degree of spiritual discipline. You won't always have the desire to read and study your Bible, nor will you have the desire to pray all of the time. Discipline ensures that whether you feel up to it or not, you stick to the task at hand. Doing this helps you maintain your desire for the word of God, rather than losing it.

*Don't you dare break down in this season of transition when you have the power to break out!*

# CHAPTER 8

# Where Your Strength Comes From

*The Lord is my strength and my shield: My heart trusted in Him, and I am helped; Therefore, my heart greatly rejoices, And with my song I will praise Him. -Psalms 28:7*

One of the keys to success in your walk is to realize that God is your true source of strength, and then allowing Him to take full control of your life. Acceptance is one of the most important aspects of surrender. When we accept that God has power over everything, even the situation that we are currently going through, life begins to feel a bit more manageable. The ultimate strength in us comes from surrendering.

Some of us are not willing to let go of our lives, we consider it too precious to hand over to God, forgetting that He is our creator, and He has our best interest at heart. We like to make plans for how our life would work out, what steps we would take in the future and so on, always forgetting to bring God into the picture. God owns all of our lives, and He can do with them as He pleases.

A story that I have always found interesting is the story of the eagle. Whenever there is a storm, an eagle does not fret or get frightened, it simply uses the wind to rise higher; and it continues to fly above the wind. As believers, how we will be able to face the challenges of life depends on where our strength comes from. Does our strength come from God, or do we believe that we are strong enough to face the challenges life throws at us alone? The Psalmist in Psalms 121:2 says; "my help comes from the Lord, who made heaven and earth." For us to be positioned to excel, we need to make sure God is our strength in all we do.

## Rejection is Not Always Bad

Some of us want the crown, but we do not want the cross. In order for you to get the crown, you must bear the cross too. When we earnestly desire something, but it doesn't come when we want it to, we should be rest assured that God holds our best interest at heart. God does not always give us yes for an answer, but that doesn't mean He does not know what we are passing through, or why we need those things we truly need. One thing we need to know is that whatever God does, it is for own good. When we do not always get what we want, when we want it, we should know that it is definitely for own good.

God knows when the perfect time is for a prayer to be answered, and He will hold on to it until that perfect time comes. It sometimes can be frustrating, thinking that our prayers may be unanswered, or maybe God is not listening to us; this is not true. God listens to everyone, everywhere; however, He is not going to do for you what will eventually harm you. As humans, we only see the prospects in an opportunity, we hardly see the danger. God being an all-seeing father knows just what opportunity holds, both the prospects and the dangers, and from this, He makes the best decision that would not hurt us.

When we need something desperately, all we can do is pray and ask for the direction of God. It is also at this stage that the Holy Spirit comes in. In earlier chapters, we have established that one of the things that the Holy Spirit does is to teach us how to pray and to pray for us too. The Holy Spirit will not teach us to ask for things that are not beneficial to our lives. However, at times when answers do not come as quick as we would have expected, all we need to do is hold Him to His words and hang on.

When God speaks, He makes promises to us. God often speaks to people through visions, dreams, speaking to people directly, and many other ways. When He promises to do something, we should know that immediately or later, His promises will come into fruition.

Abraham is a typical example of what it takes to hold on to God's promises. God told him that He would give him a son, and even as an old man, Abraham never doubted God, not even for one second. Sarah, his wife, laughed at the Angels that brought the good news; but Abraham believed. Even when it looked impossible, he still believed. This is what God expects from all believers. Unquestioned faith in God; a blind faith in his abilities. Whenever God promises us something, we try to rationalize it and bring it down to the level of logic. We tend to forget that with God all things are possible.

## Delayed but Still on Time

God's timing is the best; it has always been the best and it will always be the best. God's timing is not our timing, and God knows when best to fulfill His promise or answer our prayers. When a prayer or a promise appears delayed to us, to God it is just on time.

Many of us want to do things according to our own purpose, and according to our own actions. It is important for us to trust God completely, releasing the reign and allowing God to take over the control of our lives. God is the master planner, and the master builder; He will never lead us astray. Many times, the devil tries to make us believe that we are alone, and that God has abandoned us. No matter how fierce the storm may be, God is always with us, telling us to fix our eyes on him. If we keep our eyes on Jesus Christ, we will not lose focus. Look at Peter, he saw Jesus walking on the water, and Jesus told him to walk too; he did. Along the line, he lost focus, stopped fixing his eyes on Jesus, and then began to slip. Some of us today will begin to hear the lies of the devil, and we will start to lose focus. The devil is always on the lookout for vulnerable believers who he can return to his kingdom. We should never allow God's delayed answer to our prayers discourage us, thereby giving the devil an opportunity to attack us.

*There are many reasons why God does not answer on time – according to our human definition of "timely":

1. ***God uses it to teach us a lesson.*** If you look at the case of Lazarus, when his sister came running to Jesus about the health situation of her brother. Jesus deliberately

stayed back for some days before heading Bethany where Lazarus and his two sisters were. By the time Jesus got there, Lazarus was dead. However, the whole situation was done to increase the faith of everyone who witnessed to situation and for them to give glory to God (the whole story can be found in John 11)

2. *To teach us patience.* God sometimes delays in answering prayers to teach us how to wait on Him in the place of prayer. A lot of us want we pray for with immediate effect; we do not have patience whatsoever. When God delays, it is done sometimes to teach us patience. The scripture says; the vision is for an appointed time! God does not work with our time; we must therefore learn to work with his.

3. *To increase our faith.* Nothing increases the faith of Christians more than having to wait on the Lord to answer our prayers. A look at the Lazarus case will show us how people's faith can increase through delayed answers. A look at the life of disciples will also explain this in clear terms for us, with each delayed answer, the faith of the disciples increased.

## Keep the Faith

*But without faith it is impossible to please Him, for he who comes to God must believe that He is, and that He is a rewarder of those who diligently seek Him.* Hebrews 11:6

Faith is the ultimate test that makes us qualify as a Christian; it is what distinguishes us from unbelievers. Faith is the ability to conceive something in the realm of the spirit and bring it into actualization in the physical realm. The whole Christian journey is based on faith; no one has seen God, but we all believe He exists. It is this faith that drives us and keeps us going as believers.

Hebrews 11:1 defines faith as, "the substance of things hoped for, the evidence of things not seen." This is the perfect definition anyone can give faith, for what is faith if not the evidence of things not seen. In the contemporary world, a lot of us today are following the bandwagon of people who try to rationalize faith, bringing their understanding of God down to logic. This is not how God works or operates; God works in mysteries. He is the God of miracles, and unwavering faith. The operation of God cannot be reduced to the unravelling of our little understanding, what God demands of us is blind faith. Yes, blind faith. When God says He will do something, we should believe that He will do it. In this thing called life, don't let your problems be bigger than your faith. Do you believe that all things are possible? If not, you are denying the power of God.

Here are some miracles of signs and wonders that greatly increased my faith in God. I, myself have nothing to gain by telling you, but I have a lot to lose by not telling you the truth. The following testimonies were used by God to confirm to me that He is with me, and that he has also given me His power:

## God Reigns and the Son Shines

It was an early morning, and the whole sky was gray, almost as if a thunderstorm was about to happen. I was sitting on a 5-gallon bucket by myself, and I looked up at the sky. I prayed, "Ok Lord, try the spirit, by the spirit. You say, greater is he that is in me than he that is in this world. You said these things that we shall do and greater. Ok Lord, not by my power, but by your power I command to see the sun right now in the name of Jesus." The sun came out immediately, it was almost as though the cloud was holding the sun in its hands. And I kept looking at as it stayed out for about 35 seconds before going back into the cloud. I then commanded to see the sun again so that it could be witnessed by other people. Soon after, my co-worker, Omar, came up to me and said, "did you just see what happened?" I asked him what happened, and he explained that the sun came out and it went back in. This miracle really strengthened my faith. Some things cannot be explained, but you have to know it was nobody but God.

Omar Panetta, witness of the sun

*Very truly I tell you, whoever believes in me will do the works I have been doing, and they will do even greater things than these, because I am going to the Father. And I will do whatever you ask in my name, so that the Father may be glorified in the Son. You may ask me for anything in my name, and I will do it. John 14:12-14*

Jesus says in Matthew 17:20 that all we need to move mountains is faith as small as a mustard seed. A mustard seed is so small that you can barely feel anything in your hand if you hold it, yet this is the level of faith God requires of us to move mountains. While Jesus does not expect us to remain at the level of a mustard seed faith forever, that level is enough to do great things with the Lord. Faith is the key that opens whatever we need in the presence of God. When we have an unquestioned faith of God's power, we will receive whatever we ask for. The Bible says, "Ask and it will be given to you."

One of the reasons why God's response to our prayer is usually delayed is to increase our faith in God. Sometimes, delay in people's request brings them closer to Him, thereby increasing their faith in Him. Some of us never learn to have faith in God, unless we are faced with serious life challenges. As believers, it is important to know that without faith in God, we cannot receive anything from Him.

Isn't it something how we can finally get evidence of God's healing? Our mind still tries to tell us otherwise. I remember at time in my life that I was going through a back to back season of challenges, and the spirit led me to understand that I needed spiritual restoration, and renewal of my mind. Even though I was healed, and delivered from those situations in the physical realm, in the spiritual realm I still had conflicts within my mind. I kept rewinding the tape and telling myself the same story. I couldn't understand why I was still negative. I was living with a spirit of bitterness and unforgiveness. I was actually hurting myself more staying in that space, even after my deliverance. I now realize that at the time of my deliverance, I may have also been in the spirit of disbelief and feeling of being unworthy to be healed. My body was healed, I was delivered from my situation, but my mind was still bound. The problem was my belief system. If we do not get with the program and allow our mind to catch up with our deliverance, we will cheat ourselves out of our healing. Understand that Christ saves our souls, it is our job to put forth the effort to have our mind restored.

Think back about how many opportunities you've had in your life that you couldn't quite rise to the occasion. Were you the hold up? If we continue to stay stuck, God will show us his power through other people in order for us to believe. He probably feels like "Oh, there is evidence that the power is real. I showed you evidence. You still don't believe. Now, let me do it through somebody else. Maybe then you will believe." We as a people, tend to believe more when we see manifestations happen through other people, than when it really happens through us. When we see the manifestation of the healing power that is done through others, we can accept it better. There is a battle going on in your mind, which is why it is so important to rest on the word: "And be not conformed to this world, but be ye transformed by the renewing of your mind, that ye may prove what is that good, and acceptable, and perfect, will of God". –Romans 12:2 KJV.

## Having a Conversation with God

Works of healing in the body didn't just happen to others, but I also experienced it for myself. In one situation, I had grown frustrated at the fact that God had given me the ability to heal others. I found myself dumbfounded about why I could not heal my right leg that was bothering me. On this incidence, I was at my job working, and was having a conversation with the Lord. I asked: "Lord, why is it that I can go to a nursing home, and cast out demons out of people, and I can touch other people in your name, and they can be healed, but when it comes to my leg nothing is working for me?" The Lord spoke to me clear as day: "It's just like ordering a pizza. You have to be very specific with what you want. I could have healed your leg, but you did not say when you wanted your leg to be healed."

Wow is all I could think to myself! I couldn't believe what God had revealed to me. I needed to be specific with my requests that I brought before him. So, I went into the bathroom, and spoke out to God: "Okay, Lord. Not by my power, because I don't have any power, but by your power, Lord, I command the pain to leave my leg right now in the name of Jesus!" When I came out of the bathroom, there was no more pain. I began to shake my leg in amazement, trying to look for my leg to ache, and there was no evidence of any pain. I started to walk, and for days I continued to look for traces of pain. I didn't doubt God, but every now and then something within kept urging me to test my leg out looking for the remnants of pain. Finally, I broke down, and asked the Lord why I was walking with a limp. Immediately, the Lord said to me: "Because the Devil has paralyzed your mind into thinking that you have not been healed, and you have." Right then and there, I stopped limping. I was healed from my leg pain, never to feel it again. God truly blessed me, and it was a miracle!

# CHAPTER 9

## Don't Quit

Quitting on yourself is one of the most painful things in life. Those who have, often find it difficult to forgive themselves. People quit for different reasons. There is a sense of urgency to get things done or achieved at a certain age. It's like we are in a race against time. In this comparison society that we live in, we often compare our life's achievement with that of others. Having failed repeatedly at so many undertakings, life can become tough and often painful. It becomes boring, and the willpower to proceed seems not to be. It's easier to quit when we think over everything that has happened in our lives. You may be closer to success than you think. For this reason, you must always develop the willpower to continue to press on. Every setback happens for a reason; a setback is a setup for a comeback. We may not always know why an event or situation has occurred, but we must keep going.

Success must be earned, and to achieve success, there is a price to be paid. To quit, is to believe you deserve better when in fact you haven't earned it. Opportunities are bound to happen in life, and no one knows where or when the next one will present itself. Quitting shuts the door against these kind of opportunities, therefore adopting an open-minded spirit, is the best bet. A fulfilled life is what creates the innermost satisfaction that every man desires. No man becomes fulfilled by quitting. You never know how soon you might start seeing progress if you hang in there and give it a little more time. It takes a lot of courage, tenacity, some grit, and self-determination. The joy that comes from not quitting on yourself and achieving the height of success you have always dreamt of will give you the energy you need to overcome more incredible challenges in your life. Success breeds success.

Not quitting is key to success in both our secular, and spiritual life. Life is too short to allow the mistakes of yesterday to keep us from moving forward. God has already forgiven us, but instead we stay stuck in our guilt. We get hung up on the mistakes made several years ago, and ultimately concluded that life cannot be better for us than it already is. Soon, we find ourselves wallowing in our own self-pity. We stop dreaming. It becomes the most painful decision of our lives. Do yourself a huge favor, and learn how to stop the insanity, grieve your losses, accept God's grace, and walk with Him in the land of the righteous. Take your rightful seat at the table. You've earned it after all! Success can only be guaranteed, when you don't quit.

## All That You Endure

Contrary to what we think or the impression we hold, endurance is a virtue that can only be developed by the height of opposition we face. It is the amount of challenges we can withstand, without giving up. There cannot be endurance, without a test of faith. A level of opposition will always rise along the way to success, but that is the only way endurance is built. Trials are meant to test our resolve, and the strength of our faith. We all know life isn't promised to be a bed of roses, even roses have thorns on their branches, but the thorns don't stop us from plucking a few of them. The journey to the top will be full of ups and downs. It is endurance that keeps us moving and not quitting. When things become too hard for you, lift your hands to our heavenly father, and say: "Lord this is difficult for me, I need your help." I don't know about you, but I cannot go a day without the help of the Lord. We all need a little more Jesus! One of the ways God helps us is by giving us the strength to endure. He knows that if we quit in the face of opposition, we destroy our chances of success.

God strengthens our resolve in the face of opposition through the backing of his word. The bible says, "For with God nothing shall be impossible." Luke 1:37. What a backing we have in the word of God. When we feed on it, our spirit man comes alive, and our resolve is strengthened. When you know and truly believe that with Him all things are possible, you will push on no matter what might come your way.

You always have God, and His word to fall back on. The clouds are at their darkest when it is about to rain. When opposition is at its peak, success is around the corner. God never fails us. With Him success is always sure, only if we can endure. He sometimes allows the hardest battles in life to be experienced by his beloved children. It's called tough love. Even the Lord Jesus Christ himself was not spared. He had to endure the agony of the cross to be able to save the world from their sins. Christ was in much pain when He prayed in the Garden of Gethsemane. "Looking unto Jesus, the author and the finisher of our faith; who for the joy that was set before him endured the cross, despising the shame, and has sat down at the right hand of the throne of God." Hebrews 12:2.

Jesus had to endure shame, reproach, and agony in His quest to become the savior of the world. He had all the reasons in the world to give up, but He didn't. The bible encourages us to look up to Him as an example, and as our motivator. Hang in there, because God is always there for us when we need him!

## I Commanded the Rain to Stop, It Obeyed

While sitting in the work shed at work, it began to rain very hard. I began praying to God, saying: "Ok, Lord, not by my power, because I don't have any power, but I command the rain to stop right now in the name of Jesus!" Miraculously, the rain came to a complete stop. I walked of the work shed, and my boss Henry rolled down his car window, asking if I had just seen what happened. He explained that the rain stopped almost as if someone turned the faucet off. In that moment, I just smiled and walked away. I tell you what, that experience alone increased my faith even more. When you begin to see things like that in the spirit, your level of faith becomes unmeasured!

Henry, my boss and witness to the rain

## Purpose for the Pain

What exactly is God's purpose in allowing his children to pass through pain, if it is true that He loves us as His children? When going through testing periods in life, we often result to asking the question, God why me? What did I do wrong? God's purpose for allowing us to go through a time of pain is to draw our attention to Him, and to establish His purpose in our lives. It's like training an out of shape everyday person to become a boxing champion. The body fat has to be eliminated, and be replaced by muscles through rigorous training, usually accompanied with a level of discomfort and pain. There is always the option to give up and say, "I can't take the pain anymore". Just know that you can't have your cake and eat it too. The pain is the price you have to pay to become a champion. God has to prepare us for the future. He needs to build up our trust in Him, not in our own resources. If the purpose is going to be accomplished, then we would have to endure the pain. If you are going to become a Champion for God, you have to endure the rigors of the training.

God allows pain to prove us, or to approve us. He uses it to test our character response to adverse situations. He wants to know if we truly believe in Him, or if we are just playing lip service. Some folks give up on God when troubles come. They forget all the good things that He has done for them when things aren't going the way that they want. Well, that's why we have to see it God's way, and not our way. We must seek His will in everything we do, not just our own will. God uses pain to discipline our carnality, break down our selfish will and show us our point of weakness. Our spiritual growth could also come with a level of pain and discomfort. The pain, and the discomfort helps us to wait on God, causing us to use the promises and principles of the word. This process brings about some changes in our spiritual lives, allowing us to grow. Obedience to God is not always the easiest; it often costs us some pain as well. It can require sacrifice, courage and discipline. No matter the pain it might bring, God is always with us. His purpose for allowing the pain is always going to be to our benefit, if we let him. *"When you learn to take control of your carnal mind and subject it to obedience to Me"* ...

## You Wouldn't Believe What God Asked Me to Do

On one particular beautiful day, and while out visiting the sick, I went to visit a well-respected man in my town. Deacon Wilson was thinking about giving up on his life, because he felt as if nobody loved him. The devil had been tormenting his mind into thinking that there was no other reason to live. Keep in mind that he was a devoted deacon in his church, loving husband, and a cherished Father. He was indeed loved by many, and even I had the utmost respect for him. When I arrived, I began to minister to him. Just before I left, we prayed together, and I promised his wife that I would return in a few days to check on him. On the way back to visit him, I prayed out to God: "Lord, please reassure me that the prayer I said for Deacon Wilson has truly helped him. In order for me to know that it has, I would like him to also pray for me, so that I can have confirmation of his healing." While visiting him yet again, the enemy tried to seep into my spirit, urging me over and over to pray for him myself, attempting to cancel the plans of what I had originally requested to God. Knowing the trick of the enemy, I fought back against the devil with a bold NO in my spirit. At that moment, a television series Law and Order came on, and Deacon Wilson smiled, saying that it was his favorite show. That was my cue to leave, but before I left, he asked me to come towards him. He grabbed my hand and began to pray for me. When he opened his eyes, he confessed that he didn't know why, but the Lord had just told him to pray for me. All I know is God did it. I left his house floating on cloud nine. Boy, my God is awesome!

## Not Bragging, but Boasting on The Lord

Whenever we go through the turbulence of life, and we can come out victorious, we must realize we didn't do it all alone. We had help along the way. Our confidence does not come from relying on our own power, it comes from relying on God. We could easily be tempted into taking all the credit for the hard work done, and begin to brag about it, but the bible requires us as believers, and children of God, to do exactly the opposite. I don't brag or boast, but I do believe in giving God His honor. We simply cannot take the credit for all the He has done for us. Therefore, as it is written: "Let the one who boasts, boast in the Lord." 1 Corinthians 1:31. There is no need to brag about anything. Everything should be done to the glory of the Lord. The bible says in Daniel 2:20 "All wisdom and might belong unto God." How many times have we heard people give themselves all the credit for the good things that happened to them, only for them to turn around, and blame God when situations and circumstances are not going their way? It doesn't work that way with our Father. We hear people brag and say "Oh, I did it all by myself" or "I'm self-made." The fact is that no man accomplishes anything all by himself. There must have been a form or measure of help along the way. If we are going to boast about any of our accomplishments, our boasting should be in the Lord. It must be premise on the fact that the reason why we are celebrating to begin with is because of the goodness and mercy of the Lord. If anything, our boasting should be in the fact that He was the one who kept us going, even when we almost gave up on ourselves. "But as for you, be strong and courageous, for your work will be rewarded." 2 Chronicles 15:7.

All the praise and glory must be given to God. He will work on you one on one if you get honest with yourself and move pride out of the way. This shows that we have reached another level of our spiritual growth as a believer.

# CHAPTER 10

## Coming Out with All of the Power

During Jesus' time on earth, He demonstrated tremendous power in His ministry. He healed the sick, raised the dead, and performed other diverse kinds of miracles. He also faced His own trying times. As great as He was, He also suffered persecution, and opposition. No matter the level of opposition, His faith never wavered. Jesus was aware of the power that was inherent in Him. He knew God was the source of His power and He could always count on God at any time. "And Jesus came and spoke to them saying, all authority has been given to me in heaven and on earth". Matthew 28:18. Jesus was telling His disciples about His ability. As believers, we have the power of God inside of us. God made His power available to us, because He knew that our human strength has its limit.

We have to become bold like Jesus was, and face the opposition. I could imagine the look on the faces of His disciples when He told them that He had all the authority in heaven, and on earth. There must have been a sense of relief on their faces. It must have put a measure of confidence in them, knowing that they have a powerful master, otherwise the level of animosity shown to them by their enemies would swallow them up. One thing is certain; the word of Christ put their minds at rest, and allowed them to receive His strength. In Matthew 18:19, Jesus commanded His disciples to go and make disciples. The knowledge of the power of God inspired them. It wasn't as if Jesus was unaware that His disciples were likely going to have some turbulent time ahead, but He would rather them go in confidence, than to create fear in them.

Coming out with all the power shifts our focus to be on the power of God, allowing us to be able to see Him through in all circumstances, not focusing on the trial in itself.

## Healing from Severe Back Pain

All day long, my wife had been complaining about her intense back pain. It hurt so bad that she wanted to go to the hospital, but because it was late in the evening, she decided to wait until the next morning. When we went to bed that night, and while she was asleep, I laid my hands on her back. I prayed, "Lord, not with my power, because I don't have any power, but with your power, Lord. I command her back to stop hurting right now in the name of Jesus. Reveal to her that the back pain is gone while she is on her way to the bathroom." After that prayer, I fell asleep. The next morning, I woke up to go to work, and noticed that she was still lying in bed. I told her that I was about to leave for work. She replied: "Okay. I may still go to the hospital when I get up." Before I arrived to work, she called me, and asked if I had prayed for her last night? I replied: "Why do you ask?" She said, "Because my back is not hurting anymore." (What I really wanted to know was when did she find this out.) I asked her, "When did you find out that your back wasn't hurting anymore?" Her reply was: "On the way to the bathroom this morning". "On the Way To The Bathroom." She never ended up going to the hospital after all, and to this day, she has not experienced any more intense back pains. To God Be the Glory! God is so amazing. Let me tell you, when God tells you that you are endowed with His gifts, His power, and His authority, He will show you real evidence. He will give you eleven witnesses, so that he can prove to you that HE IS WHO HE SAYS HE IS. There is no way that you can say that God has revealed Himself to you, or has given you certain types of gifts, but you have no evidence that He has given you these gifts. He will always come through and deliver!

## The Finish Line, I Can See It

*"I press toward the goal for the prize of the upward call of God in Christ Jesus". Philippians 3:14.*

The greatest decision you can make is to never give up, and to rely on the strength of God to see you through. The finish line is like being in a marathon; after running a few miles, you turn the corner and there it is. You can see it from afar. The energy experienced in the final few meters at the end is intense, and being able to see the finish line always does something to an athlete. No matter how weak or tired we may be, crossing the line becomes a must. The one who is running in a marathon, will not get distracted. There is only one focus. The finishing line. Not all who run in a marathon race are really interested in winning, some run as a hobby, some run to stay in shape, but others run for the purpose of accomplishment. You and I belong to the latter part. We press towards the finish line, because life is a race. A marathoner may be running on a 20-mile-long marathon, but they are not thinking about what happened at the 5th mile or what may happen at the 10th mile, the only thought that crosses their mind is about crossing the finish line.

The apostle Paul was a determined believer who would not be deterred with the finish line. He wasn't going to quit no matter what. Not even when he knew the persecution that was awaiting him, all he saw was the finish line ahead. In 2 Corinthians 11:24-25, he gave examples of the terrible circumstances he had been through. Paul speaking said, "From the Jews five times received I forty stripes minus one. Three times I was beaten with rods, once was I stoned, three times I was shipwreck, a night and a day I have been in the deep". This was the magnitude of opposition that arose against him. Ours might not be like that of the apostle Paul, but as believer and children of God, we face oppositions nonetheless. In the book of Acts 21:4-12, a prophet of God called Agabus came to Paul, and told him about things to come. In verse 11 the bible says, "He came over, took Paul's belt and bound his own feet and hands with it. Then said, "The holy Spirit declares, 'so shall the owner of this belt be bound by the Jewish leaders in Jerusalem and turned over to the Gentiles."

What a revelation. How many times in our trying period, have we had people come over and tell us more about our problems, without giving us any helpful piece of advice or a solution that leads to a way out? They try to discourage us, telling us to stop fighting and give up. Some even give us examples of their failed experiences, trying to dissuade us from seeing the finish line right in front of us. Thank God he stood by us. His opinions about us, and the situation should be what matters the most. The apostle Paul was able to press on towards the finish line. He was able to make a bold declaration in 2 Timothy 4:7, "I have fought a good fight, I have finished my course, I have kept the faith, I have finished the race." When we get to this point in our Christian walk, we will look back and thank God for how He has seen us through the turbulent periods of our lives.

## No Longer a Blurry Vision

Receiving a God-given vision to run with is one thing, having the needed faith, perseverance to accomplish such vision is another thing. Having a clearer understanding of what the vision entails is very important. When God gives a vision, he doesn't give you all the details of the vision all at once; that would be overwhelming for many of us. As you journey along with Him, He begins to make your vision clearer, so that His purpose for your life will become revealed to you. It's difficult to effectively pursue a vision that has not been made clear. Just know that God will never leave man in doubt as to what is plans are, and where he is taking him to. Everything will eventually begin to become clear unto us when we continue to trust God in our walk with him.

*Let Me remind you, my child, that My burden is light. It is light because you are not supposed to carry it on your own. My Spirit is the One who carries it. Each time you take things upon yourself, you will wear yourself out.*

God gave Abraham a vision, but he was unclear about how the vision was going to become accomplished. The vision was blurry. Genesis 15:5 reads: "Then he brought him outside and said, look now toward heaven, and count the stars if you are to number them. And he said unto him, so shall your descendants be". He had to believe God and move on. In Genesis 15:6, the bible says, "And he believed in the Lord; and he accounted it to him for righteousness".

As Abraham continued to journey with the Lord in faith, the vision became clearer to him. He had to have some faith to persevere. The vision would not become clear unto him, until some years later. In Genesis chapter 18, Abraham out of the goodness of his heart, decided to attend to the needs of some strangers, unknown to him that it was the lord that was visiting him. No wonder the bible called Abraham a man of faith". You see, faith is a fruit of the spirit, which is to be employed even when the vision of God for your life looks bleak and blurry. As you stick with God employing the use of the fruit of the spirit, He will reveal certain things to you so that you will not be in doubt or in a state of confusion. An understanding comes with such revelation, which inspires into you a heightened level of confidence in God, just like it did to Abraham. Whatever might be the God vision or purpose for your life, don't quit. Have faith, endure, persevere, and seek the help of others. Employ the use of the fruit of the spirit and the vision.

# CHAPTER 11

## Mature Christian (Philippians 1:9)

As you continue to develop in faith, you will gain a new understanding that God's aim is for us to develop into full maturity, and to be fruitful for Him. The journey of our lives involves consistent growth, growth only stops when we have stopped breathing. God expects us to grow continuously. The best way to grow into full maturity is by feeding our soul and spirit the word of God all the time, and also by submitting to the teaching of more mature believers. As we continue to grow in the faith, we will get to know more about God. However, as we grow in faith, so does temptation we will face and the battles we will fight get stronger.

### Taking a Punch, and Using It as a Push

In our journey through the world, there will be people who will seek to distract us from our goal, trying to lead us through the path of destruction. However, when we make the Bible our companion, no one would be able to sway us from our goal. Many of us will miss it, because we are so fixated on getting it right through our own knowledge without ever relying on the Holy Spirit. Once we realize that by our power we can do nothing, we shall be able to stay on track and achieve our goals. The inability to cling to God is the reason why most us find it difficult to fly above defeat. When we allow the Holy Spirit to guide us, every defeat will be used as an opportunity to plan again and re-strategize for the future. The Bible makes us understand that our enemy is a lion roaming, seeking whom to devour. When the Bible says the devil is looking for whom to devour, it does not only mean that he is seeking those to destroy and kill physically, he is also seeking those he can destroy psychologically, mentally and spiritually. When the devil fails at killing you physically or spiritually, he tries to kill you psychologically; he wounds your mentality. Many of us have been wounded mentally and we just remain in that defeated state unaware of anything we can do to salvage our situation.

In life, we must always rely on the Holy Spirit to help us bounce back whenever those around try to punch us and try to keep us down. Every adversary must be seen as a lesson God wants us to learn. A lot of times we trust our parents or our friends or anyone close to us; we trust them to keep their promises, we trust them to make sacrifices or us, we trust them to attend to us anytime we call them. It often happens that when we need them the most, they fail us. They didn't fail because they wanted to disappoint us, they failed because they are humans and not everything is within their control. Most times, God uses that situation to teach us a lesson that He is the only one who never fails. When these things happen, and we are bedeviled with failed promises and disappointment, we need to push on and put our faith in God, the one who never fails. Stop putting so many expectations on people to do the things for you that only God can do for you.

As true disciples of Jesus, we need to take things as they come, and not react negatively towards people when they challenge us. When they punch, we need to use their punch as a push for us to go higher. If we consider the lives of the apostles, they were tested and persecuted several times, but that did not deter them, it just became a push for them to work for the cause of the gospel even more. As followers of Christ, we face a less severe form of persecution, however, no matter the amount of punches we get, we must never let it keep us down. Again, when we make the Bible our ever-present companion, we can learn from the experiences of the heroes of faith and make our lives ultimately better.

## Advantage over the Adversary

Once we pledge our full and total support to God, we become a target for the devil and his agents. Every Christian, no matter how mature you are, is susceptible to the attack of the devil. The devil is never after the salvation of our soul. In fact, the devil is forever after the destruction of the human soul, forever on the look for souls to take into his kingdom. For everyone that believes, the kingdom of hell gets depopulated and the kingdom of God increases; for everyone that believes, the devil loses a soul. For this reason, the devil is always looking for ways to win back the lost souls.

First Corinthians 10:12 tells us to be aware if we think we can stand so we do not fall. The reason why Apostle Paul warned the Corinthians is because he knew that even though they accepted the message of Christ, the devil will be forever on the lookout to sway them to his side. Nothing has changed about the devil since apostle Paul wrote the letter to the Corinthians, and the warning is still relevant today.

Since we have found a new peace in Jesus Christ, we know the devil is going to attack. The good part of it is that we know we have already defeated him even before the battle starts; we have gained unrestricted access to the power of our Father. With this power, we can fight the devil and defeat him. Some of us aren't even aware of the power that we have as sons and daughters of God; for this reason, we have allowed the devil to control us. The truth is, the devil has no power over anyone who has confessed Jesus; he can only be granted access when we sin. It is therefore to be known by all who believe in Jesus and are called by the name of Jesus, they have defeated the devil already. All we need do is to tap into the abundance power of God, operate under the Holy Spirit, and keep pressing on to greatness.

## The Miracle after Attending the Sid Roth Supernatural Show

Joan Gieson lives in an atmosphere of miracles!

On Thursday July 20th, 2017 I was a guest on The Supernatural Sid Roth Miracle Explosion program. Joan Gieson was a guest, sharing stories of serving in ministry with Kathryn Kuhlman, supernatural faith healer. Of all people, Joan called me out of the audience, saying: "The glory of God was on my life." She laid hands on me and prayed for me. Then she prophesied that I would be able to perform supernatural miracles. Words will never express the feelings, and emotions experienced at this show. I was anointed in the power of Jesus!

Joan Gieson lives in an atmosphere of miracles!

On that following Saturday, I drove to the bank. As I stood in line, I listened to a sermon in my headphones. I was also standing in line beside a young man, and he began talking to me. At the time, I couldn't hear him, so I took my headphones out of my ears, and I said "Excuse me sir. Did you say something to me?" He replied "Oh I'm sorry, I know what you mean by that. I'm deaf in my right ear 100%."

At that time, I asked him if he believed in miracles. He told me that he did, because I was a preacher. I told him about my previous encounter at the Sid Roth Show with Joan Gieson, and how she passed the mantle to me to perform supernatural miracles to the lives of others. He became excited and interested to know more. When we were done with our banking transactions, we met in the lobby. I began to share with him some of my past divine encounters that I experienced throughout the years. In that moment, I looked down at my hands, and we both saw the anointed oil flowing through my veins. I showed him that I too have the hands of Jesus, and he asked me to lay hands on him, and pray for him. I took my right hand, and I put it on his good ear, then I put my hand on his head and prayed for him. The young man then asked me to pray for his bad ear. I took my right hand and cuffed his deaf ear, and after I prayed for him, we walked outside to continue our conversation. I walked up beside his deaf ear and began to whisper a prayer in it. I stepped away and asked him if he could hear what I said, and he amazingly repeated to me everything that I said to him! I quickly reminded him that I thought he was 100% deaf in his ear. He replied "Yes I am, I was. I'm standing here now wondering how I was able to hear you, and I know I'm deaf in this ear." I said you have just been healed in Jesus' name!

## Give Yourself Back to the Lord

*Present your bodies a living sacrifice, holy, well pleasing to God, which is your reasonable service. -Romans 12:1*

Jesus said I did not come for those that are well, but I have come for those that are in need of a physician. In Ecclesiastical 7:20, the Bible says, "For there is not a just man upon the Earth that doeth good and sinneth not". No one is perfect, however with your flaws, inequities, and imperfections you are the perfect choice. I encourage you today to make God your perfect choice. If you would like to give your life to Christ today, repeat this prayer out loud, and confess "Lord, I know I'm a sinner, and I ask for your forgiveness. I believe Jesus Christ is Your Son. I believe that He died for my sin, and that you raised Him to life. I want to trust Him as my Savior and follow Him as Lord, from this day forward. Guide my life and help me to do your will. I pray this in the name of Jesus. Amen." He is knocking, will you let Him in?

When you sacrifice, your reward will be that much greater. When we are saved, and born again with the life of God, we must keep in mind that it is only the beginning of something new and beautiful. Your new life is on the other side of salvation, and during your spiritual journey, please bear in mind that you will have to move forward step by step. Rome was not built overnight, so understand that neither will you. It all takes time. Sometimes you will go two steps forward, and three steps backwards. The beauty is in the willingness to be obedient to keep going. Stay focused on the prize of God, pray for strength, and unselfishly give yourself back to the Lord. When we are regenerated during our life long spiritual journey, giving ourselves back to God allows us to be a living sacrifice, and to consecrate ourselves to him. This is the hour where we can't just talk about our walk with Christ, but be about it. Jesus healed 10 people at one time, but only 1 came back and said thank you. Are you one of the 9, or that number 10? When we give ourselves back to the Lord, we are confessing "Father God, use me. I am no longer for this world, myself, or anything else but you. Let your will for my life be done." Allow God to use you for His satisfaction.

Why do I need to consecrate myself to God, you may ask? We should be willing to walk in the Lord's way. Before our salvation took place, we chose our own direction for our lives and walked in our own way. When we consecrate ourselves back to Him, we allow the Holy Spirit to lead us into righteousness. Another reason is that consecrating ourselves allows us to surrender to the Lord, providing the best opportunity for God to grow and develop within us. Growing in life and being divinely led allows us to grow internally and externally. In the spiritual realm, we ultimate grow deeper in faith. Even before we can go on to help others, and be a vessel for God, the Almighty needs to work within us.

Being saved is only half the battle. We must keep up the effort to have God work through our "mess". When the true word of God is spoken, you will see a change in your behavior, your thought process, and your spiritual tolerance. From our thoughts, to temptation, lust, spirit of fear, rejection, oppression, bondage or afflictions we all have work to do. Your anointing is there, but so is the spiritual warfare and strongholds. Denying our flesh and being obedient enough to allow the Lord to work through our fleshly desires and shortcomings will ultimately give God the glory once He is done with us. Wholeness for you is on the horizon, just you wait and see.

God is a gentleman, so understand that He will only work on you if you allow Him to do so. You can be a saved Christian for many years yet have little growth. If you want to make a radical change in your newfound life, consecration is the way to go. Allow God to go to work on your behalf and use you for His purpose. Give Him permission, and pray to Him "Lord, I want you to work on me, and in my life. I give You permission to have your way with me. Help me to heal and be delivered from my shortcomings. Conform me to be who you need to be, Lord. Lead me by your Spirit into the purpose for my life." Will you recommit your life to Christ today? Let the Lord take you by the hand and lead you into a consecrated lifestyle. He will be your strength and give you the grace to walk it out.

Here are some ways to get started: cut out any unnecessary distractions, clutter, and temptation. Receive God's grace to walk it all out, as you cannot do it all by yourself. You need the Holy Spirit's help to guide you. If you make a mistake, be sure not to beat yourself up, forgive yourself, pray for forgiveness and keep moving. Live in expectation that you will reap God's positive consequences for living a consecrated life. You are rich in joy, love, peace, abundance, health, and wealth. Start living like it each, and every day. Be intentional about your consecration efforts by fasting, praying, and tithing daily. Make the most of your mornings by being intentional. Wake up earlier than everyone in your household and spend time with the Lord. Ask the Lord to reveal to you where should you go, what you should do, and to whom you should sow into. Do an intermittent fast throughout your day, and exercise your spiritual muscles by practicing gratitude, and meditating on a scripture each day. Journal your spiritual thoughts when needed and go back to the Lord to reveal more in-depth revelations as you go about your day.

It is my deep prayer that you will not only be saved but resurrected and reemerged from the ashes with a new will of desiring a consecrated life, with the understanding that it is going to take will, tenacity, and resiliency on your part. There is beauty in your ashes! I cannot say that since I have been consecrated that my life has been a walk in the park, but what I have come to understand is that the things that I once loved has been slowly becoming what I least desire. The transitioning has been very challenging, but the transformation has been worth the change. I have learned that on this journey, your life is not your own; once you realize that, you will find out that God can do a much better job of taking care of you than you can. Everything is not going to happen overnight, it surely is a process that you go through on this journey.

Consecrating your life back to God will be the best decision that you could ever make in your new spiritual life as a follower of Christ. There is nothing more fulfilling than living wholeheartedly for God in this lifetime. Our greatest God-given privilege is to seek the Lord with all of our heart, and hunger after God. When you give God your all, your life will be transformed forever. You will never be the same person again. When you live a consecrated life, there will be an overflow that will allow your light to shine so bright that there will be no denying that God has done His work in you. You will truly be living for His glory, and it is in those moments of transition that you will have the authority to operate in divine power.

As you continue to fight for your healing, freedom, and salvation, remember my friends, deliverance does not mean done. Your work has not come to an end and is not to be taken from granted. Deliverance simply means that you are now aware of what's going on, and you know the difference between continuing to stay stuck or not. As our young kids today would say: "Stay Woke". While being aware of your challenges, understand what it takes to be suited for spiritual warfare. Being delivered does not mean it is over; in fact, the war has just begun. You have overruled what the enemy has thought he defeated you with. Once you have been revealed of the things that you are dealing with, you will know how to handle obstacles, and opposition as the journey becomes more challenging. The weapons of our warfare are not carnal, but mighty through God. Your biggest fight that you will ever fight is in your mind.

If you live by the spirit, then love by your heart, renew your mind, and then ye shall have the power. God is able. He's able to do all things but fail. If there is ever a time to fall, it's when he wants you to fall in line with him. This is the season that the Lord is going to turn things around in your life. Now that you are equipped with the tools necessary for the shift, remember that all praises go to the glory, and honor of God. I pray your strength in the Lord. Never stop praying, and never stop believing that the power lies within you. May God bless you real good!

*But ye shall receive power, after the Holy Ghost is come upon you: and ye shall be witnesses unto me both in Jerusalem, and in all Judaea, and in Samaria, and unto the uttermost part of the earth. -Acts 1: 8*

For booking inquiries, and correspondences, please contact us:

www.PGLMinistries.org

PassionGLMinistries@gmail.com

Facebook: www.facebook.com/PastorGregLink

Made in the USA
Columbia, SC
28 September 2020